# The Elements of Heaven

*Meditations of Univernatism—
The Formulae for Life*

RJ Widry

WIPF & STOCK · Eugene, Oregon

Wipf and Stock Publishers
199 W 8th Ave, Suite 3
Eugene, OR 97401

The Elements of Heaven
Meditations of Univernatism—The Formulae for Life
By Widry, RJ
Copyright©2009 by Widry, RJ
ISBN 13: 978-1-5326-9953-5
Publication date 8/20/2019
Previously published by Publish America, 2009

*Sad are the bearers*
*Of other men's burdens*
*Simple are sowers*
*Of goodness and Earth*
*Wise are the knowers*
*Of freedom and dungeons*
*Rich are the Spirits*
*That value their worth*
*Bless'ed are those who have*
*Weathered the price*
*For they follow on way to Paradise*

# Chapter 1

The major premise for this work rests within the understanding that Life includes various *formulae* for joyful and harmonious existence. These formulae are both Natural and Universal, yet are experienced differently by *each individual* (hence the word: *Univernatism* indicating the *Universal and the Natural)*. As an apple is an apple each person who eats one will taste and react to it in his or her own individualistic way. However, the elements and properties that make it an apple are established. Thus these formulae have definite and established elements and properties that constitute their formation. One of the assertions I will propose in this work, is that these formulae are each presented to us as Natural properties of life. I will also be describing natural and universal attributes of existence that surround and support the formulae.

If presented with an apple one might eat it, or cook it or perhaps plant its seeds. As with the formulae we each have our own way of organizing their value and determining their place in our lives. If we attempted to make an apple into an orange we would find the experience to be frustrating and futile. Although we determine the actual contents and value of the formulae as individuals, certain essential elements cannot and should not be changed. We will discover as we explore the formulae that they *do* require a definite order for us to follow. We will also discuss the consequences of *not* following this order and the personal benefits bequeathed to us if we do oblige these formulae their specific ways and design.

I have chosen to represent the aspects of each formula by their *initial letters*. As the components are such *things* as "Knowledge, Love, Relationships", their specific rendering would be known as: K=Knowledge, L=Love, R=Relationships and so on. I have found this type of symbolism to be particularly helpful in both Meditation and Conscious *organization* of the formulae.

*We can begin with the Formula "KES" or*

## Knowledge—Experience—Sight.

The *knowledge* represented here is that of *External* origin, meaning those events that are (or have been, i.e. our *memories*) perceived and reacted to which originated in the external environment. *Experience* is *internal* as *Sight* is. By sight I am referring to: the way in which we *see* something, or sum something up, make a conclusion about it or evaluate it. By this understanding I am *not* referring to our *physical eyes* rather it would be our mental perception of what our eyes might be seeing.

The knowledge that we might be aware of could be something that is either pleasing to us, or displeasing. We may now explore some basic human encounters wherein our own KES will determine their effect on us.

We see someone that reminds us of someone else. The person he or she reminds us of is someone we like and have had a good relationship with. The *knowledge* of this person's existence comes from an awareness of the *physical world* in which they (and we) are living, the *experience* of seeing this individual is felt *internally* as we react to their being there. The *sight* arises as a mental projection created by the knowledge and experience of their presence. If the individual we see reminds us of someone else that we happen to enjoy then the completed KES will be pleasant as the *sight* will fulfill to be an evaluation we can accept and hold within us. The *experience* will of course be influenced by our *remembered experiences* of the things we shared with our friend, allowing for the end result or *sight* to be pleasing.

This is an example of a Whole KES. Wherein there were no conflicts or unresolved issues involved or stimulated. A whole KES would include our ability to *contain the sight* in an understandable and acceptable way.

Suppose we then see an individual that reminds us of some person who we are not particularly fond of and perhaps have some unresolved issues with. Again, following the *Natural* course of KES we come to *sight* and we are unable to complete the encounter. We cannot embrace a complete mental understanding of this encounter because the *experiences* we have had with this unfriendly person are not resolved.

We might even shun or ignore this person's innocent greeting to us because of our unresolved KES, and later wonder why we were rude to them.

Our KES's are vital for our Life. They are "keys" to the understanding of us. Had this unresolved encounter occurred to someone who was involved in a life Meditation, he or she might return home and contemplate the confrontation. By looking into themselves and retracing the path they might discover the reason for the negative sight that led to the rejection of this innocent passerby. By allowing themselves to realize that this person reminded them of another they could address the problem in a productive way. By working with themselves they could be able to create *sight* that would include seeing others as *their individual selves* even though they reminded them of people they have or had problems with. We can each "work with ourselves" by creating and developing helpful guidelines for self-learning/teaching following are examples of certain rules and liberties that we as self-teachers can adopt:

*Be ever patient with yourself*

Allow for self-forgiveness as you Sincerely, Purposefully, openly dedicate yourself to learning, changing, growing. By understanding that perfection is gained not given we can agree that past problems we might have caused for ourselves are each part of the learning/growing process.

*Inexperience is not a crime*
*Ignorance is not a mistake*

*Only if one consciously and knowingly does*
*wrong is he or she culpable for the act*

Do not be picayune and harp on yourself (this type of "self-finger-pointing" cannot really be either productive or instructive. We each need to learn how to become our own best friend, accordingly we should become benevolent self-teachers, being unlike those pedantic schoolmasters who we have learned only to resent and refute) By adopting and adhering to Patient, Lenient, Tolerant rules and liberties of our cerebral classroom we can create an inner atmosphere and ambiance conducive to learning and growing.

*Do unto yourself as you would like others to do with you.*

By initiating this type of inner work room we can *broaden* Sight while accomplishing internal resolutions of certain problems. In this way we would have a greater number of whole KES's as we grow to understand more about ourselves and life itself.

When next we see someone who could recall in us an unpleasant experience we might instead smile (even to ourselves) as we consider some of the humor of being human. If so, then our sight would have grown to include this type of encounter making our quest for happiness that much more realized.

Upon further investigation into the two incidents, the pleasant and unpleasant one, we might conclude that Experience alone determined the outcome. But this conclusion would be incomplete and therefore erroneous. Experience determined the *inclination* of the outcome, as an internal force, but the combination of Experience and Sight determined whether it was pleasant or unpleasant. This understanding creates a distinct and vital difference for our approach to KES. That which we have experienced *cannot be changed*, no one can alter the past, but the way in which we See or contain the past within us can very well change. In this way we can make our lives better and if not actually change our past, we can resolve or redress it. Our present condition and future prospects rest in our ability to learn from the past, resolve that which needs to be resolved and expand our individual Sight. All of this is possible.

As well as being Universal and Natural Spirituality Univernatism attempts the syncretism of Spirituality with psychology, an East meets West endeavor. "Psychespirituality" would be an appropriate word for the formulation and incorporation of psychology within a Spiritual practice. Furthermore I do feel there is a genuine need for the joining together of psychology with spirituality because of certain missing elements not found in each of these important humanistic subjects:

Psychology itself lacks any spiritual teaching and/or guidance within its doctrines. It would be of great benefit to those seeking psychological help to be able to draw upon certain spiritual understandings and tenets in order to assist in developing and creating an harmonious existence. However, within the practices, teachings and (certain) tenets of spirituality exist, I believe, ideas that are basically psychologically *unhealthful*. Therefore by giving a spiritual nod to the reality and insight of psychological study, spirituality or psychespirituality could open, allow for new avenues of greater health and happiness.

In addition, as incredible as it might seem, and it does actually seem incredulous to me, the etymological, literal translation of the word *psychology* according to its origin in the 16th century is: *study of the soul*. Even so psychologists and those working in related fields i.e. psychiatry, social work, mental health counseling etc. are loathe to acknowledge or address anything *metaphysical*. Most often these professionals categorize metaphysics in clinical terms and more likely than not they would diagnose rather than discuss the metaphysical experiences of their clients. One purpose many of the proverbs that I have written, and follow keep is to be a verbal nexus, a connective statement joining two or more insights, truisms into one cohesive thought. To that end, and by way of addressing this current subject, psychesprituality, the following proverbial assertion should effectively address and connect, in a syncretistic manner, psychology with spirituality:

*Whatever is good for the emotions, consciousness or psyche, is right for the soul as well*

By working with and focusing on Experience and Sight when we are dealing with KES we *will grow*. To simply reject unpleasant incidents as unworkable without examining their construct or possible resolutions would be a willing decision to stop growing. We would then have to make arrangements so that we would never have to confront certain unpleasantries, this in turn would limit our individual freedom.

The purpose of this work is to assist in the creation of happiness and fulfillment by describing, explaining a more Universal and Natural approach to understanding Life.

\* \* \*

In order to comprehend, discern (more exactly) the meaning of "Universal and natural" according to Univernatism we might need necessarily to define what is not. For quite often within this type of arcane, esoteric discourses "shedding light through opposites" becomes a valuable and helpful tool. Accordingly, we might begin with the more exoteric debate of "Subjective v/s Objective". It is most generally accepted that subjective ideas, opinions, points of view are biased, not unbiased, prejudiced by personal experience, not open-minded, egalitarian. Objective considerations are conversely conclusions or observations that are fair, candid and straightforward. Although I will not assert that the objective equals and is Natural, Universal, these statements should bring us to a place where we can work towards understanding the Natural, Universal. As well I would point out that "subjective ideas and/or conclusions" being by definition arbitrary and specifically personal viewpoints can definitely not be seen as being conclusive within the realm of the Generally accepted ideology of the Natural, Universal.

If indeed the reader is satisfied that these statements fulfill "the burden of proof" for the assertions made within the treatise then by way of prima facie we can continue on to the next step as: "how does one get from the Objective to the Natural, Universal?" By incorporating the synonym "innate" for the word Natural we may be able to facilitate the process. Thus our innate inclinations, predilections are part of our Natural selves. The "law of self-preservation" is a prime example and useful now in the discourse.

*Somehow the hardest law for people to follow is the Law of Self-preservation*

At this point I shall assert that following the law of self-preservation is a Univernatistic approach to Life, and is part of the Natural, Universal. Furthermore, "following" would as well indicate an exhortation to: act upon, choose, and adhere to. Therefore being self-destructive, choosing to do that which would be counter-productive and against one's best interests is not actually Natural. In my estimation I shall assume and presume that for the reader to agree and acknowledge these assertions as being valid and bona fide would not be calling for "a leap of faith". As such, this then would be the step, the bridge, where the Natural is defined and the Universal is indicated. For assuredly whatever would be verified as natural innate for one or more individuals must be Universal and applicable for all.

Reflecting now upon this treatise and in order to further the understandings and import of the definitions herein I would introduce at this point another widely known exoteric debate: Nature v/s Nurture. Return with me now, if you will, to our discussion anent: subjectivity and self-destructiveness. I feel quite confident in declaring that self-destructiveness is not part of our basic Natures. For I feel equally, if not more, confident that there has never been nor will there ever be a case, an instance, whereby after being born an infant goes directly on to committing suicide. The unresolved inner-conflicts that develop and manifest as we face difficulties, without answers, in life are the cause for external acts of self-destruction and/or counter-productiveness, hence: Nurture not Nature. Albeit this is an example of unhealthy "nurturing", but never the less it does shed light upon the discussion and allows for an evaluation of the healthy v/s the unhealthy. For indeed I believe that the Univernatistic approach to life is definitely a healthy choice thereby endorsing Univernatism as an ideology to be espoused. Obviously there does exist a place in life and Nature for our subjective selves but that place should be internal and in harmony with our external existence. Our internal, subjective selves should not nurture unhealthy conflicts that metastasize into external acts of self-destruction. Although they are all too common, unfortunate and in a sense "understandable" according to this dissertation these acts are unnatural, pathological. Individuals who are experiencing subjective inner-conflicts need first to objectively recognize them as such thereby overcoming a state of denial. After this objectivity is gained the path to one's true Nature becomes more illuminated. Thusly the progress and process follows as: subjective-objective-Natural, Universal.

Although mightily simplified this paradigm should shed light upon a goal of Univernatism.

*  *  *

In this way, prejudicial or judgmental observations are avoided and refuted while humanistic and objective approaches are created. In nature there exists an acceptance of the past, a way in which we help to resolve difficulties that have occurred by simply accepting the reality that they have occurred. I have learned that:

*One cannot forget the past until it has taught all that it can teach*

I have found this to be a type of *Law of Life*. Experiences will continue to affect our lives until we have effectively learned to incorporate them within our lives. Then they become a part of us, they become our teachers and not our enemies. Our personal inclination towards new or growing Sight is a needed attribute for development and resolution. Working on Experiences with a willingness to See a conclusive and positive ending will afford us much opportunity to see fulfillment.

We might think that we are protecting ourselves by trying to live by an arrangement whereby we would avoid certain encounters. Let us look at the word "protect". An enclosed cell can protect but its isolation from external reality makes it unhealthy. That which is basically unhealthy is not truly protective. Eventually the shortcomings, whatever the unhealthiness is, will wear away the protection. Metaphorically this *cell* could represent a person's internal encasement. An emotional or intellectual shield often *protects* grief or unhappiness felt within. Within the confines of this type of individual construct one might decide to simply discard the apple that is offered by making the conclusion that it is not a desired thing. The decision to be open-minded and explore life and the determination to reject some part of life are examples of *personal laws*. For the purpose of examining more fully the

Formulae for Life and their inner workings we can define and discover aspects of personal laws. Personal laws are the rules that we have created for ourselves and try to live by. Internal lawmaking is a common and natural part of life.

\* \* \*

By these statements we would be able to define or compare the word law(s) as being: (like) a conclusion, a summation of ideas, the consequence and culmination of specific facts or datum. Obviously we each are the sole body that would pass and implement these laws, hence: The Legislature.

Our own governmental legislature, Congress, has to (or is supposed to) follow the guiding rules of The Constitution when passing laws. As such The Constitution is the "written Aegis" that governs the governors. Consider then if you will what would make, or constitute a "good law" for us as opposed to (not a bad law per se) a law that cannot work well. Is it possible to construct a guiding Constitution with General Principles that we each can apply when creating our specific laws? By recognizing the reality that the two main forces behind the creation of laws are actually: Psychology and Philosophy we then can be able to create guiding Principles. The essential understanding of the relationship between the two, Philosophy, Psychology, rests within the more perfect working order of their placement, hence: which should come first? If one allows their personal psychology to affect their own personal philosophy the effect is a self-serving idea, or law, that has no Universal or Natural properties or attributes. Therefore I would assert that: Philosophy needs to overrule Psychology. In light of all this following is a written guide, Principles, for the creation of personal laws:

*Philosophy over Psychology*
*Philosophy with Psychology*
*Philosophy guiding Psychology*

As we continue with the subject of personal laws perhaps the reader would be able to glean which of the following, mostly recognizable, laws are created according to these principles.

Undoubtedly these laws are made from the lessons experience and life itself has taught us. "I will *never* do that again", is a common law that many do adhere to. Usually this is a good thing; it arises out of making the same mistake enough times that we've promised ourselves not to repeat it. Some personal laws are not as healthy or protective. "I will never let myself need anyone ever again" or "I will never let anyone again see what I really need or am feeling". Our individual laws will affect the workings and outcome of Life's formulae. These rules can either assist or impede the creative motions that exist within life itself. "I will allow for growth and inner development" would be a type of law that could move with you as you travel through life. By not making a dead end, an intellectual *cul de sac*, we would leave more avenues open for joy.

If we institute laws of non-interaction with the external world, our internal worlds can suffer. We would be unable to See the fulfillment of a KES if a restrictive personal law was significantly influencing our Knowledge of events taking place. As we are the sole body that enacts personal laws, we can repeal them. An internal act of easing self-imposed restrictions could come from a KES as we See a more amenable way to live.

Within these understandings comes the realization that *conscious knowing* affects and is part of K=Knowledge. Truisms we have accepted as valid, proverbial insights that we see as realistic and true parts of life will each have an influence on our general conscious knowledge. Learned personal laws and acknowledged axioms about life are components of any individual's conscious mind, affecting their perceptions and decisions. If someone believes that; "all people are created equal", their evaluation of other individuals will be more tolerant and liberal. They might teach themselves *laws* for being *non-judgmental* as they move through society. If someone believes that: "it's a man's world" this idea will affect his or her perception of fairness. If male, he might give himself the right to do that which a *ruler* is allowed and believe himself to be justified. If female, she might be overly sensitive to male dominance or control sensing an unfairness in the way the world works and is constructed. She might pass the personal law that it is right to be rude to men given their "high and mighty" position.

The actual reality or trueness of these laws and proverbs is questionable, given that they are each *subjective* interpretations of life. By nature a truism or proverb needs to be an objective understanding about life that can be applied or adopted by a majority of individuals. I would hope that my readers have taken note of my efforts to write and construct truisms and proverbs within those guidelines. Rather than disseminate a subjective view as a worldview, I consider non-biased discernment to be worthy of distribution.

As we examine the personal laws and proverbs that affect Knowledge we can see those that help and those that hinder. The individual who rejected the stranger's honest greeting was affected in part by his or her personal Experience. But had they held to some type of personal law or proverb that *allowed or encouraged* rudeness there would be less chance of them becoming more open or friendly. Their Experience that caused a predilection towards a negative response was complicated and reinforced by supporting ideas.

*You make something better by not making it worse*

Had they learned perhaps to: "give someone the benefit of the doubt" when meeting an individual whom they have no prior history with, they would improve their chances for new friendships and harmony.

This new understanding could begin on their arrival home while reflecting upon the incident with the passerby. What would be the KES here? How could it work? Within the introspection arises the realization of the identifying of the stranger with the person they know. This recognition in itself is a KES. Here the Knowledge is about an occurrence that took place in the physical world. After recognizing the *source* of negativity i.e. the past Experience, their Sight would be *moved* to open some. We are now discussing the process by which a more open and tolerant KES can be created. While Sight is set in motion the negative Experience could also *loosen* and not have such an inflexible grip, internally. The Meditator could then *let go* of the Experience allowing for a positive and healing contemplation. What we are describing here is in fact two *internal motions*: the first being an *opening* of Sight, the second a cathartic *releasing* of Experience.

"Perhaps I could have seen or reacted to that differently", as Sight opens allowing for new possibilities. With support for this "new way" coming from a release of Experience, the conscious mind can adopt a different proverb or law. "I'll be less prone to reject others" while seeking the possibility of friendship and mutual understanding.

These ideas are creative and will help improve a wide range of relationships. A new and whole KES has been created, centering the individual with purpose and direction.

*Experience is the Teacher, Knowledge the Liberator and Wisdom the Master himself*

As we examine the reality of Motion within the gears of KES the ideas of Balance and Co-ordination become relevant. Universally speaking, is the Meditator seeking balance and order? Is the search for harmony a Natural part of existence? Was this in fact the *deciding element* that allowed the whole KES to be formed? While internally debating the pros and cons of letting go and opening to new ideas, was the Universal external world somehow involved? Encouraging our individuality to behave as the Universe does, with Order and laws of motion, we acquiesce to this exhortation giving in to a more harmonious way of life.

While the wheels within us are spinning, attempting to find a way that works, the unbeknownst effect of Universal forces are helping our decision process. Beautiful! We *do* have something watching over us! A design that each of us can identify with. A harmonious order that recognizes our searching and helps steer our individual paths. A Cosmos that reacts as we react, offering some wise advice from an ancient Source. "Learn to flow with it", "be more open to change", "expand your horizons". Who would argue with such Benevolent suggestions?

That we all are subject to certain laws of nature and universe could be explained by relatively simple examples and observations. Such as: if and when we get hungry or thirsty none of us has the inherent, internal ability to create food and water just because of our natural needs. We must rely upon the external world for our sustenance; I call this reality "a natural inability". If we simply do not want to eat or drink we cannot make ourselves "not hungry" or not thirsty that would be unnatural and impossible. These illustrations should be sufficient in pointing out some of the natural laws that we cannot circumvent. Why would we want to? Life works much better if we simply "follow Nature's call" and attempt to satisfy our needs by natural means.

Similarly, the Universe maintains definite rules as it governs the order of life. For instance: suppose we are hungry and near an apple tree but the apples are far on top upon thin branches. We cannot simply jump the 30-40 feet in the air and grab apples. Gravity and natural inability will prevent us. But we could incorporate the external world's tools and get a ladder.

Some might think it would be much greater to build an elevator to get to the fruit. But what an effort! I do not believe that in this case constructing an elevator would be either prudent or warranted. Therefore the *more simple and direct* approach is actually the better. Like the Zen master who suggested to his student that it would be preferable to cover one's feet with cowhide rather than attempting to cover the earth in order to avoid being hurt by sharp stones, wisdom has traditionally sought the less difficult choice.

We each would benefit by accepting Universal and Natural laws and working within the limits of our abilities when attempting to solve a problem or gain satisfaction.

Much Goodness is all around us, but like the forest and the trees many seem not to recognize it. As well people have a tendency to make life more difficult then life needs to be. Perhaps they agree with their response to passersby, that they should ignore and reject unasked for greetings or assistance. While a Universal Goodness watches and suggests, but does not interfere, certain individual KES's operate separately and alone. "Nice guys finish last", "take whatever you can get", "make up your own rules". Yet, one individual was able to create a more positive and workable approach to life. He or she had had difficult Experiences that affected their Sight and worldview. This person formed a positive and whole KES by re-examining their conclusions, lending themselves some needed influence and input in order to improve their lives. The result was a brighter and more open view of life and the world. A lighter outlook which could perhaps See a Universal Goodness that rests in place. Was this a Door? Was the Meditation that allowed light in, actually a turning of a Key that partially opened a portal to Universal Truth? If so, what other valuable realities rest in Light as we search for the meaning of our existence?

An individual who believes in Universal Goodness could be called a pantheist, or an exponent of the Philosophy of Optimism reckoning that Goodness will eventually triumph. An Epicurean or a hedonist could each embrace a doctrine that declares Cosmic Magnanimity. The latter two philosophies maintain *pleasure* as their central focus. Whereas an Epicurean would most likely be a Bon Vivant, indulging in the pleasures of the palate and such, hedonism embraces a wider range of pleasures. Believing that "whatever is pleasurable is intrinsically good" a hedonist would live as a pleasure seeker, feeling justified in acts that stimulate the senses. I have heard that Rome was born Spartan and fell Epicurean as pleasure seeking, and self-justification eventually eroded the political and social systems. Internally the "eternal city" could no longer stave off the sieges around it as it became increasingly divided and diffusive.

This historical and philosophical datum gives a clear

indication of the importance *pleasure* has had on our Earthly chronicles and Humanity's development. I do not attest to the hedonistic doctrine that defines the relationship of Pleasure and Goodness. I do feel however that:

*Whatever is actually goodness is also pleasurable.*

This statement is not merely a change in the juxtaposition of words, for by holding the prime subject to be *Goodness*[1] rather than Pleasure the meaning has a very different import and indication. If one were to truly believe that whatever pleases them is good, what prevents them from seeing the harming others as good if they enjoy executing revenge? Would they consider the harming of themselves to be a benevolent act if they derived some type of pleasure from it? Perhaps it was ideas such as these that contributed to, or actually caused the fall of Rome. Because *pleasure* was *put before goodness* an empire fell and the world was thrown into the Dark Ages. What an ironic and amazing idea!

If we were to say, and hold as a proverbial ideology, that:

*Goodness feels good to us, but we respect Life*

The transposition of the subject with the inclusion of a simple clause makes for a wonderful rule that we could live by. In a general KES about Life we could See Goodness as a

Constant making the rejection of Goodness the thing to be concerned with.

*Nothing is essentially bad, what would be wrong would be the denial of that which is Goodness*

If we hurt others we are denying the Goodness of Life and its call for preservation and respect. If we hurt ourselves then we are denying the Wisdom of our inner voice that urges us to be Good to ourselves. Somehow the seeking of pleasure, which seems to be a simple and natural thing, has caused historical and personal catastrophes. Hedonism by its definition in modern psychology holds that: "Behavior is motivated by the desire for pleasure and the avoidance of pain." We could magnanimously attribute painful situations that others or we have endured to errant choice making while *intent and motivation* was good. We *were* seeking a pleasurable outcome for others, or ourselves but "it" did not work out that way. With much of our day-to-day existence involved with some form of pleasure seeking and satisfaction we could utilize some type of guide that could direct our behavior.

The ideas stated below could be used as reference for certain KES's when the Sight sought for contains a fulfillment of pleasure:

*Type*(of pleasure) *Determination*

Pleasure that is
*against you*..............................avoid...forego

Pleasure *for you*
but *against* others......................beware...resist

Pleasure *for others*......................can cause problems
but *against you* do not encourage
(sacrificial)

Pleasure *with*
*and for you*...........................good...accept...support

Pleasure with/for you
plus *with others*......................excellent...develop

Through the descriptions that follow we can work towards mutual understanding:

Pleasure that is (in fact) against you:

This would indicate that which is self-destructive such as overindulgence in drugs or alcohol. Pleasurable or comforting as they might be for the present, with their sedative and life numbing effects, they can cause much harm. If we use alternative substances as substitutes for real solutions we will not experience actual resolutions.

Pleasure for you, but against others:

In the end these types of momentary pleasing experiences are not really *for* you. The vain satisfaction one might feel after carrying out some vengeful act will not create happiness. The satisfaction often can turn to feelings of guilt or remorse as the effect on the object of revenge is contemplated. Even a sense of unworthiness can follow this act of triumph, as one wonders about the merit of an individual who would engage in such deeds. With self-discipline and understanding we can resist temptations to lash out at others. By containing for a moment what might actually be *just anger* and firmly but without malice confront the cause of this anger, the results can be rewarding. Instead of harming another, or our relationship with others by seeking the pleasure of revenge, we can deal with certain situations more fruitfully. Perhaps we *are* indeed justified in our anger, but if we can explain our position, pointing to the reason for our resentment, we might avoid damaging a potentially good friendship. Furthermore, relationships that *have survived* angry exchanges that were pointed but controlled often become stronger and more valuable.

Pleasure for others but against you:

To please another by making some type of personal sacrifice is understandable and benevolent. But if we continually go out of our way for others, eventually we will lose enough of our force of goodness that it will be spent. Some try to please others because they fear rejection. Thinking that if they say "no" to a request they will lose a friend. People such as this often find themselves in relationships that demand much but offer little in return. A real friend *will accept* a "no" as an answer if a good reason is given. To act out of fear of rejection is *not an act of love* it is a reaction to fear. The proverb that states: "It is better to give than to receive", is logically imperfect, for if this were a truth then everyone should give and no one should receive. By reorganizing the concepts and motions involved and including Natural reactions in Life we could state that: *It is best to give then to receive.* The process of giving and receiving creates balance and replenishes acts of goodness with goodness allowing for further benevolence to take place.

Pleasure with and for you:

Engaging in some form of self-satisfying experience is healthy. Treating ourselves good is goodness. We can make the world look and feel better if we give to ourselves that which we enjoy and deserve. We should know ourselves the best. Within this knowledge is contained the understanding of what pleases us. We can and should act on this knowing, providing for ourselves that which we will enjoy as opportunities present themselves.

Pleasure with and for us plus with others:

Interacting pleasurably with others is one of Life's greatest rewards. Sharing the joy of living with those who share your views is wonderfully pleasing. Without taking away from anyone else we can share the experience of pleasure contentedly. We should develop and nurture those relationships wherein these kinds of exchanges can take place. Therefore the creation of an individual paradise, although challenging to be sure, rests within the vision and will of individuals.

## *Philosophies of Paradise*

There are doctrines writ by men of woe
Which bruise the mind and confound the soul
While claiming to expound the truth
Declaring union as their goal
The dogma of the circular reason
Thrives on defining, then proving itself
Creating the rhetoric of treason
Words betraying Man himself
Aware in the light of a perfect day
The philosophies of paradise truly explain the way

Subjective vision can never be
The eyesight for humanity
Nor can one find peace of mind
In the confines of morality
On the pathway of ascent to truth
Obstacles may confuse
For the barriers and binds we see
Are oft mistook for reality
But the real is truly bounteous
Providing safety, satisfaction
The philosophies of paradise
Express the meaning of salvation

Laws are meant to give fair guidance
A protective foundation for Man's benefit
With clauses that free, and exceptions that we
May apply if conditions demand it
Happiness is everyone's right
Unity is everyone's work
Preservation is life's basic need
Humanity seeks to be freed
The problems we face are solvable
If the answers are jointly sought
The philosophies of paradise
Are in essence, God's lessons taught

The receiving of Pleasures, natural and healthy, is an essential experience and necessary for the creation of happiness. Although pleasures by *themselves* cannot bring us to lasting happiness, they do remain as needed aspects of everyday life. As we have discussed the insidious hazards present in an over-emphasis or an over-indulgence of pleasures, we can consider what the effects are of *unnecessary denial*.

By using the Formula KES to examine the inner workings of someone who tends to deny him or herself pleasure we can project a scenario such as:

An individual has enough food and an appetizing desert to

satisfy his or her hunger and needs for the night, but no more than that is available. Two friends arrive unexpectedly and after some pleasant conversation it is discovered that they are both hungry. The two have enough money to purchase a fine meal at a nearby diner but because it is cold outside they would rather eat the food that is presently available. The person whose home they have entered does not get paid until tomorrow afternoon, and he or she does not have enough money to buy a meal. Within this person's "K" is the full awareness of the circumstances. But while he or she is *searching for* the right course of action the experience of guilt rises. Being aware of the visitor's hunger and knowing that food is nearby the person denies themselves needed sustenance giving much of what is in the house to the hungry guests. After consuming the food, leaving not nearly enough to satisfy their friend's hunger they offer a sincere thanks and leave. Hungry and disgusted the person gets a modicum of rest and has a difficult day at work.

    The Knowledge of his or her friend's hunger combined with the Experience of guilt disallowed a Seeing of a more just solution. This was an incomplete KES that led to much difficulty. The individual being unable to form a resolute decision that would be fair to all those involved wavered and then gave into the most *obvious and available* solution, giving away the food. His or her Knowledge of the situation was influenced by *past lessons* that had *taught* the feelings of unworthiness. In this way the Knowledge was already moving away from ideas of fairness and equality and towards the concept of sacrifice.

The denying of oneself of that which is needed and fair to receive could manifest in numerous ways. There are a number of things an individual would need in order to change and rearrange this type of behavior, many of which we have already discussed. By projecting the same scenario with a different individual who *has* developed the whole KES's required for a fair conclusion to these complexities the incident could be described as:

After he or she becomes aware of the friend's hunger Knowledge works to assist in the situation. This individual has already dispelled and released ideas of unworthiness by re-examining the circumstances that had caused them. Realizing that while he or she was an impressionable youth criticisms and judgments from others had a negative effect on them. Believing then that the critics were right ideas of unworthiness were caused. However while traveling through Life and achieving gratifying things a sense of accomplishment was formed. This sense along with an ability to *objectively* re-consider past criticisms and judgments encountered was enough to relearn ideas about Self, creating in turn a general feeling of Self-worth.

With conscious knowing already leaning towards just conclusions that *include* satisfying his or her natural needs, feelings of guilt were quelled. The "S" of the whole KES contained an appreciation for friendship so that rudeness or rejection was not considered to be acceptable. By candidly explaining the situation to his or her valued friends, in an open and mildly self-effacing way the end result was shared laughter and full stomachs. The visitors decided to eat at the diner and the individual's belief or whole KES that "true friends are understanding" was reinforced.

After acknowledging that we as individuals have the right of free will and the ability of choice making in given situations, we can admit that we might have misused those freedoms to our disadvantage. These self-defeating decisions could have taken place not only in our physical lives and actions, but in our intellectual calculations as well. Although KES is formed internally, the formula does connect to *three-dimensional* life by way of influence from and interaction with the external world. But because of the introspective nature of its parts, it is up to the individual how artfully and conscientiously the integrity of the formula is made and kept. As one travels intellectually and emotionally from K to E to S much opportunity for carelessness or unprincipled decision-making presents itself. Given that the lesser side of human nature can include both laziness and impatience these traits could likely appear when people are dealing with internal problem solving and self-understanding. Wanting or yearning to get to a good place in life we are ever tempted to smooth over or block out that which seems to be in our way. We need to closely examine what the consequences are of causing malformed KES's by attempts we might make to either thwart or cheat the formula's required order.

Life itself is multi-dimensional, being at once internal, external, subjective and objective. Because of the many faceted and often difficult aspects involved in the formation of KES and in life itself, it remains mostly understandable that there would be those of us who would elide over and leave out certain essentials. However, because of the uncompromising, yet benevolent, laws of Nature and Universe errant decision-making in regard to the formulae and life will cause problems for us. For instance suppose someone mentally and emotionally forms the formula as "KSE", this misconstruction might actually be quite common. There are, in fact, basic, elemental reasons for this phenomenon. Happiness is felt within as an internal experience. It is a feeling all of us wish to reach and hold. Because of a strong desire to *see* happiness in our lives we might be willing to sacrifice the very order that life itself has established for the experiencing of joy. But nature will not compromise her essential laws in order to fulfill our personal wishes. Thus happiness is felt internally *not externally*.

By forming the formula as KSE what a person does essentially is to attempt cheating the natural progression and go from Knowledge directly to Sight then try to "see happiness" externally. To further illustrate this design we can reexamine one of the scenarios we have discussed and attempt to locate a KSE.

As:

When the first individual felt guilty because he knew that his friends were hungry he looked immediately, perhaps even reflexively, to *Sight* for the answer. That fact can be discerned by noting that while he was "searching for the right course of action" the feeling of guilt became the deciding factor. Thus he "saw a way out" and rather than explore and examine his emotions he chose to simply give away the food and go hungry.

From the K of his friend's condition to the S of an immediate solution, he could have then "mentally progressed" into believing that he would "see the Experience" of happiness (externally) once his friends were fed. This was an example of a KSE.

This scenario illustrates also the impatience and lack of personal commitment present within some individuals. The end results of the one incident where KSE was in charge of the person's decisions were hunger, lack of rest, and still guilt for that problem was not addressed either. Given that the original situation was fairly benign, involving only some hungry friends, we could wonder at what dire circumstances a person's KSE could lead them into.

By following the second scenario and keeping in mind that this individual has resolved his past problems we will be able to understand how a KSE can change, be straightened out, to become a harmonious KES. We can note that the second person had experienced feelings of unworthiness and guilt, but had managed to work them out. In order to do so he would have had to face them, productively. Perhaps after going hungry and tired one too many times he passed the personal law "I will never do that again" and the next time guilt arose he dealt with it, rather than looking for a way out. Even as we examine that process or discipline of: being in touch with what we are feeling as we search for an answer, but don't *act* right away, we can see KSE changing to KES.

*In a moment of indecision the Wise do and say nothing*

By continuing with the discipline and the process the second person eventually realized that he could say no. That was the KES needed, for he *saw* that he could explain why he was unable to give his friends food and knew that they would not reject him. The subsequent feeling of happiness he would have experienced within him, after he successfully and effectively dealt with a very problematic situation, must have been quite gratifying.

*Happiness is the Foundation of Life*

Scientifica potentia est and the power we gain from knowledge of self is indeed quite potent. Thusly this solipsistic source of epistemology must be inwardly guided even as we acquire it. We each need to stay the course using the ground gained for the similar purposes as what had taught us these lessons in the first place. As we have learned lessons of love and in turn understood life and ourselves more perfectly we need to use that knowledge and power still for love and life. We may *expand and support* our love, self-love and love of life with the newly realized potency acquired from "K" and "KES" but we mustn't become recidivistic. To relapse back into taking from life and others using our newfound powers of knowledge to enhance this unfortunate and imperfect endeavor is definitely *not* the purpose for knowledge gained. Through (self) encouragement of creative purposes that serve life, our lives we will continue to help ourselves reach full individuality.

## *Pale Paradise*

Pallid paradise
Scintillate this soul
Bring the morning mist to melt
The moisture of the eye
Let the tears of faded dreams
Sputter in the sky
So joy can come from fluttered stars
Of moments let to die

Pastel Moonman
Smile to my glance
Bring me to your heaven
So I may feel the grace
The ornamented sentiment
Of laughter on my face
And warm a wicked world below
With its silicon embrace

Wistful love
Shine upon my sights
Enchant me with the mystic touch
Of lips upon my soul
Neither let my dream become

*THE ELEMENTS OF HEAVEN*

A sorrow-soiled goal
Nor ever leave my quest
To start too young
Nor end to old

(Author's note: this poem was first written when I was 16 years of age)

*Peace is Life's foundation*
*Love is learning's root*
*Questions garner hunger*
*Wisdom grows the fruit*

# Chapter 2

A foundation is a starting place from which we build. Either directly upwards or expansively in varied directions, our foundations need be solid in order to support our growth. Once we have built then expanded or risen to a point in life where we feel a need to share our accomplishments with others, we seek out sympathetic individuals. These natural and universal insights bring us to the second formula: **FAR** or Foundation~Ascent~Relationships. As a natural and instinctive progression in life we first build then ascend then share ourselves with others. I can see the workings of *FAR* in almost every aspect of our lives. We learn to walk then talk and immediately begin to *ascend* by way of *expanding* our vocabulary. The first words most of us learn are for *relationships*. Mom and Dad and whoever is in our lives at the moment are recognized and named thus creating a more communicative relationship with them.

Even before words are spoken the act of ascending by standing upright i.e. learning to walk, then moving towards our helpful guardian is an example of FAR.

\* \* \*

Curiously and importantly we can find an example or an allusion to FAR even in 2000 BC. As I have "seen" these formulae as inherent principles in Life their actual "existence" becomes, perhaps, even more genuine upon examination of "Oedipus'" famous answer to the" Riddle of the Sphinx":

"What is the creature that walks on four legs in the morning, two legs at noon and three in the evening?" The hero Oedipus gave the answer, "Man,".

By way of explanation and extrapolation the first part "four legs" is a description of a crawling infant or **F**. The second part: " two legs at noon" is of course consistent with the natural progress we have just discussed i.e. "ascending, standing upright" thus **A**. Lastly the "three legs" indicates Man walking with a cane hence: **R** Relationship whereby we "lean on others" or develop helpful alliances as we travel through Life.

\* \* \*

After a solid education our foundations are made for our life ascent. We would "come up in the world" by landing a good job then develop relationships with our co-workers. Again FAR is in operation as a natural way of life. As with KES, the formula FAR does require personal discipline, prescience, and dedication for us to gain positive and lasting results. We would only experience unsatisfying or problematic outcomes if we attempted to force or elide over the natural order and progression of the formulae. For instance, if we *did not* gain the needed foundation of a good education and tried to ascend to some high paying place of employment without it, our relationship with that place and the personnel present would not work out. Eventually our shortcomings would become too obvious and we would need to find a position elsewhere. Similarly if we do not spend enough energy or effort to ascend well we will be crawling amongst others who are walking tall. The apprentice becomes the master through training and dedication. By accepting the requirements for graduation, and following those essentials, he or she will become an accomplished individual. Thus by attempting to defeat the purpose or progression that FAR requires, we would do that which was self-defeating.

In relationships themselves the ways of FAR is evident and important. Typically we would not say that we have an actual *relationship* with someone that we said hello to while passing by. This could have been a *foundation* though, for if we happened to meet them again we could refer to the previous incident using it for a friendly introduction. Afterwards we might wind up sharing a meal or a drink and then begin to develop a rewarding relationship.

But if we saw someone on the avenue that we did not know at all, had not made even the basic contact of a passing greeting, the effect of suddenly accosting them and asking this stranger if he or she wanted to have dinner would be too shocking. Even the most gregarious and outgoing individual would have to wonder about such an event.

These examples illustrate the general necessity of following the natural progression of FAR reasonably and faithfully. If we skip school, our work will suffer. By not acquiring or accepting certain social understandings our relationships with others will not reach their fullest potential.

There is another problematic development that can occur in relationships because of the liberalness and permissiveness within our modern society. Suppose the two who had dinner or a drink together after furthering their original contact found that they were attracted to one another. After a congenial and open conversation wherein each party had honestly shared their experiences with the other, assume they decide to go even further and wind up having a sexual encounter. Is their *foundation* strong enough, after only one friendly meeting, to support a sexual relationship? Perhaps loneliness and the need for comfort made having an intimate meeting that much more appealing to them. But did they rush into something and damage what could have been a true romance? Not that I believe that anything specifically *wrong* would have taken place in this example, but something unwise and self-defeating might have occurred. By not following FAR more faithfully and allowing their *mutual foundation* to be strong enough and developed enough to support and nourish an intimate relationship they might have denied themselves the pleasures of it altogether.

After waking from their one night of intimacy the awkwardness and discomfort of the moment could prevent any further moments of romance to take place. They would part thinking of how they could effectively avoid one another so that the memory of this incident could be mostly forgotten. The *foundations* within their relationship were not sufficiently developed through the sharing of satisfying general and social experiences. They had not gone to the movies, or theater together. Or watched late night television while holding hands. Experiences such as these shared over a period of time while they got to know one another could have helped create an *inner* foundation from which they might choose to *ascend*. Then after the greater, more sensual pleasures experienced during an act of physical intimacy, they would each have their own memories and personal experiences to call upon in order to make their relationship a pleasant one.

Like its physical counterpart an *ascent* in life requires a degree of ability. To rise from one point towards another in life, necessitates the use of a certain amount of internal energy. This energy can be either negative or positive, causal or creative depending on where one seeks to wind up. Whereas physical ability rests within the actual efforts employed in our acts and actions, an *internal* ability would be like the impetus or inspiration for those deeds. Those who are within eyesight of the doer notice an external act performed through physical exertion. Internal energies can be used to "rise above" someone mentally, or rise above a difficult situation by calling on inner strengths. The positive efforts put forth through inspiration could lead us to beneficial outcomes. Thus, the goal of reaching true harmony would naturally require a positive or creative source as its impetus. Friendship and understanding would also be served best through a more consonant effort. By feeling inspired to reach a worthwhile goal that objective holds fulfillment for us, it contains a satisfaction we will appreciate when it is realized.

THE ELEMENTS OF HEAVEN

# *Stranger's Satori*

I have awaken'd on earth to an alien world
Wherein all words are gems and each gate is pearl'd
The Phoenix today flew over maizefields regrown
Wherein Pixies had danced and Hobbits had twirl'd

As I marvel upon living phantasy
A marble Pygmalion speaks unto me
Though the phrases are foreign each meaning is known
So I pet the Chimera and feed the Jabberwocky

The Moon and her Mate play'd dice with the sky
So full of amazement and amusement was I
All through the night the dies had been thrown
'Till the dawn and the dew dared up the Flutterby

Right from the cocoon it metamorph'd bright and bold
Then went feeding upon the buttercups' gold
The sunlight awaken'd the Sphinx as it shone
Who upon all fours went telling tales never told

It read from the works Alexandria had lost
These words far past priceless were gain'd without cost
With all this about me I am never alone
'Midst the Guild of the Lily and Paradise gloss'd

Conversely, by displaying base or negative energies towards a desired outcome we cause ourselves to be aggressive making the end result an act of aggression.

By simply shouting out "Hello there!" to an unknown passerby, without even attempting a civil introduction, we cannot hope to create an opening for friendship.

If we were seeking to repel others and keep them at a distance, then aggressive and negatively causal energy would work. If in search of a creatively rewarding outcome then creative and positive efforts would benefit us, especially as these results include relationships with others. These understandings would be in our *foundations* our fount of knowledge whereby ideas can spring up and lead us to gratifying outcomes.

Life holds all manner of pleasures and fulfillment for us; our approach to life should be congruent to our goals. I would not express concerns for mores or morality in a work of natural and universal ideology. Those social lessons are mostly subjective and largely cultural, differing from family to family and nation to nation. But I do see life as having and maintaining certain *rules*, which when followed lead to satisfaction and contentment. For instance, would we truly enjoy something we may have stolen, taken or do not actually deserve? Would there be a real sense of fulfillment created if we lied about our education so that we could land that high paying job? Perhaps one would sit smirking at his or her boss, laughing to him or herself until they were found out and dismissed. But a true sense of fulfillment cannot come from cheating life.

*One cannot enjoy Life, whence they have taken away from it*

We can build our foundations with true knowledge and insight as we ascend with positive energies in order to create relationships for happiness and rewarding fulfillment. If we knowingly and willingly take away from life, from our lives, when do we stop? At what point does our loss become too painfully evident to ignore? Suppose two individuals lived as neighbors. One had an apple orchard and the other grew oranges. Both were perfectly satisfied and fulfilled by what life had to offer them. The apples and the oranges were all that they needed, and the fruit was plentiful and free, all they had to do was nourish and protect the orchards. When eating a delicious apple the neighbor felt pleasure and fulfillment while the natural fruit nourished with goodness. The orange gave the other neighbor a sense of contentment, safety and well-being.

One day however, the neighbor who had the orange orchard was peeling the skin off of one of his fine fruit. A wind was blowing and a piece of the rind happened to catch in the breeze and blow over to the other neighbor's orchard. Because the orange grower was so focused on the pulpy fruit he did not notice that a piece of rind had landed on his neighbor's property. But the apple grower saw the rind land on his soil. As he looked over to his neighbor, the orange grower happened to look his way too, and smiled broadly. He was thinking of how wonderful life was, providing so much nourishment and reward for them. But the apple grower mistook his neighbor's contented smile for a derisive grin, believing that he was smirking at him because a rind had fallen on his property. Angrily and with negativity the apple grower plucked one of his fruits and threw it at his neighbor. Astonished and annoyed the orange grower yelled at his neighbor, who then continued to throw his precious apples across the yard. Plucking them violently and with no thought of his preservation he continued until one whole tree was devoid of fruit. By this time the orange grower had run off in order to warn his other neighbors of the dangerous person who lived near them.

After his fit of rage he looked upon the empty tree, where he had taken the fruits from using them as weapons against his neighbor. He then realized that in order to make up for his loss he would have to do extra work and plant another tree. Also he would need to cut back on the amount of apples he ate a day so that he would not run out before the new tree could bear fruit. He had caused loss and made life more difficult due to a misunderstanding.

His foundation of knowledge and insight, at that point, had not included self-control. Nor had he worked to truly develop more of his creativity that could serve to monitor and guide his actions. As a result his relationship with the things he needed in life was damaged, and loss occurred. But in as much as he did live in an apple orchard, there was plenty of time to reflect and learn, while he planted some new trees and used necessary disciplines in his eating habits.

## Restoring Paradise

*Eden was paradise, as paradise is knowledge*
*Rich with rewards, free from dualism*
*To gain oneness within, growing without*
*Forbidden fruits of materialism*

*Innocence knows the value of love*
*Value whate'er would bring you to joy*
*The errant way is happiness lost*
*Caused by vain cunning one would employ*

*The road back to paradise, happiness regained*
*Is paved with experience, if the outcome bore fruit*
*If one lives in the world confounded, confused*
*Wisdom would point to the soul-freeing route*

*To be free from regret is recompense done*
*To be rid of devices is insightfulness gained*
*To develop compassion is selfishness lost*
*To understand errors is living explained*

*Search still the Heavens, Divinity's abode*
*They have not forgotten, you are not ignored*
*Perhaps God was waiting for Man to mature*
*For then he might cherish paradise restored*

*The child within is knowing enow*
*To recognize light that would heal and instruct*
*There need not be a schism 'tween man and divine*
*The barriers, naught but the world would construct*

*Partake of the fruits our Creator provided*
*Grow fields that reach out plant joy-sprouting seeds*
*In the gardens of Life man still might behold*
*Those golden Apples of Hesperides*

How can we apply the formulae of KES and FAR in our lives creating harmony and fulfillment? By discussing the *theory, practice and methods* of application we can discover ways by which we would be able to work with the formulae themselves. For instance, as KES is a *natural progression* in life, by understanding our inner natures we can use this formula as a guide for learning about ourselves. Theoretically the wholeness of KES should create a feeling of well-being and balance. The process of completing the K and E *with* the S creates a sense of harmony that is both strengthening and pleasant. KES is akin to Understanding in this way it naturally completes and fulfills those questions and quests for answers that are important to us. If we needed food or drink the realization of where we could readily find this sustenance would create a feeling of security within us. Similarly, when certain important and central questions about our lives are answered feelings of security and self-confidence are naturally created. Within this peace of understanding exists also a sense of happiness, for now we are more able to guide ourselves in a less confusing life. Thus, the key within KES is the *final Sight* that makes sense of, and resolves whatever the Knowledge and Experience(s) were that was troubling us. Each KES would require different practices for completion, but: *To know our Questions is a blessing* for this gives us a direction to focus our Sight towards. We would then be practicing the recognizing of the *subject* for contemplation. By noticing that certain subjects within us i.e. a person, situation or event causes discomfort or disharmony and cannot reach a Creative Sight for us, when brought to mind, we come to know that this area needs our attention.

Nature is harmonious, pleasant and pleasing, in balance. The theory of KES brings out the ideology that if we learn to *become natural* in thought and understanding we will create a pleasant harmony for our lives. By knowing our questions and guiding our answers towards natural conclusions we will become natural and One. Nature, by itself, is self-sufficient. There can be no doubt really that Nature does not need Man in order to exist. Through this understanding we can trust that we ourselves can be our own answerers in KES.

Furthermore, when working with a subject of contemplation we need to be careful not to make some *physical object* i.e. a person or event the actual *reason* for the problem. Blaming the outside world for the troubles within us is unreasonable and mostly unworkable. Truly the *source* of the problem(s) lies within our *reactions* to the physical world, they (our feelings) do not originate in the (external) world itself. However there has to exist some actual (internal) reason for our reactions. Nothing reacts without some type of stimulus acting upon it as a catalyst. Although there really are no *right or wrong* reactions per se, there are those that we enjoy, dislike or can change eventually.

If something or someone causes us to feel troubled, our K and E cannot find a harmonious S, we can work to mitigate or creatively resolve this discomfort. If we forgo *focusing* on the person or place as the *cause of the problem* understanding that they are the *catalysts* for disharmony, we can work more ably to understand the actual reasons for our uneasiness. As well, we need never blame ourselves for feeling or reacting a certain way. Self-reproach and criticism are not helpful teachers for our paths to fulfillment. If we openly accept the fact that we do feel a certain way while realizing that ultimately we can work this reaction out of us, our focus and attention will be balanced. The approach to a problem is as important as the (true) understanding of the problem. Without self-criticism or external finger pointing we can develop a compassion for ourselves as we grow. This compassion and self support is in itself part of the overall answer.

After recognizing that the K and E do not meet an acceptable S, a method for resolution is needed. We should ask our selves "Why?" What is it that we are seeing or not seeing, about this thing that prevents it from being a completed part of our lives? Why can't we simply complete the Sight creatively, what is the actual reason(s)? You might find yourself trying to *cause an answer* by attempting to force yourself to see the thing in a certain acceptable way. +—+' is not a good or workable method. We cannot just see things the way we want to and expect to achieve fulfillment. Though it might be more convenient or less demanding, forced sight is basically unrealistic and therefore unnatural. If we want to see the apple as an orange, eventually this coercion will have some ill effect upon our conscious lives. Thus, the most productive methodology would include self-honesty and awareness. Being aware of the fact that the resolution is obstructed by our *inability* to creatively See the answer, for we are, because of personal reasons, unable to complete the picture in our minds or in our lives. We cannot creatively, naturally make it wholesome for us. As we continue to explore the difficulty itself, we can recognize where and how we had looked at it. At what place in our lives had this problematic situation ended up. Where did we see it lead to, or were we ultimately unable to see an end result. These are all clues for us. Life is a great mystery, but what adventure rests before us and within us! By developing an approach of being self-interested, motivated to learn and grow we will feel better about problem solving. If we came to recognize that it was the person we dislike that caused us to shun the passerby, as we had associated him in this light, we might then try to understand why we dislike that person in the first place. Maybe they remind us of things about ourselves that we are not particularly fond of. If so perhaps we should look into those things. If we don't like them, there must be a reason for our reactions. If there is dislike there is almost always a counter-part, that which we do like and appreciate. If we dislike rudeness then we would naturally enjoy politeness, amenability. If we are not too fond of others who are over-friendly or fatuous we would find serious-minded people and conversations to be satisfying.

These methods would be followed by certain "How's" and "in what Ways". By knowing why we dislike something we can then make an intelligent search for those people and places we would enjoy. A change of one's life and environment that requires discovering new friends and locations demands both *internal and external* force. Internally we must work through the aforementioned process of recognizing and accepting our own personal preferences. Our particular likes and dislikes that we might have not paid enough inner attention to. Externally we would need to separate, say goodbye to familiar but unsatisfying acquaintances in order to find, develop truly rewarding friendships. But *wherever you go, you go with you* thus if you find the old problems occurring, arising within the new situations with the new set of people, then you probably had focused too much on external reasons and need to re-examine the problem in search of Inner Creative Sight. It can't *always* be the other guy's fault this is unrealistic.

While KES is part of nature and our inner natures, FAR is a more Universal and External formula. Originating within us, as our foundation, it extends out, up and around involving our physical environments. At this point we can see Relationships as being akin to *Place*, and *somewhere* that we are seeking to Reach. From our F of foundational knowledge we Ascend up and out in order to reach a place of happiness and fulfillment. Because that *place* is *not isolated*, one would *withdraw* into isolation not ascend towards it, we look for others to share our life with. Being further drawn by the people in these locations i.e. talented, wealthy or appealing individuals, we can work to build an F and learn to A more gracefully and effectively for our entrance into our chosen Relationship/Place.

As KES is self-contained by nature, holding our individual K, E and S within us, FAR acts as a motivating plan for our commune with others and the external world. As if the Universe within us was being called by the Universe we live in, around us, we answer with hope for rewards. We will all greatly consider, deeply reflect upon, just where and how we will find those rewards in life. Whether they take a consciously tangible form as wealth or fame, or the intangible consideration of finding love, we are each summoned to search and explore. To find, reach, discover that place or person that we can complete our lives with. As the S of KES creates an inner completion for us, the R of FAR is our external fulfillment. Thus the actual relationships we form are central for our lives.

If there existed within someone's F the inability for self-control and a negativity that went against self-preservation their A to Relationships could be quite hazardous for them. I see the need to Ascend, as just that: a need. Neither a fanciful notion nor an imaginary point but an actual necessity we all feel. A need to rise up to a certain point in life, a calling we will all answer in one way or another even every day. A cup of strong or gourmet coffee will bring us to a needed point so that we might enjoy or accomplish something. Jogs, an invigorating workout, we each have our own preferred way for ascent. But for those individuals who are isolated from society or somehow self-destructive the A can be an overuse of drugs or alcohol that leads them into a very difficult place in life. With negative support from others there, in that dangerous place, their R's can either keep them there or hinder their getting out.

Yet A is a natural motivation, and can bring us to a wonderful place in life. Thus the central or actual problem rests not in the seeking of ascension or *height*, in fact ignoring this basic need can lead to difficulties, but the why and how, the *way* in which we ascend is the key. The desire to take drugs, the dangerous habit of drug abuse has at its core a natural and healthy motivation. Drugs and/or alcohol chemically cause individuals to experience a highness an ascent. I believe the fact that the habit or craving actually stems from a basic, inherent and potentially salubrious drive complicates and causes the problem of substance abuse to be the extraordinary social ill that exists globally today. Albeit misused, misguided and hazardous if and when abused, the actual motivation to use psychotropic substances originates within a natural part of our beings. If people were encouraged to ascend towards a good place, rather than kept down somewhere dark and disquieting, society would be able to cure many of her ills.

By following the ways of FAR, understanding that it is a Universal and worthwhile part of life, we can address certain situations effectively. Self-expression is ascent, as with music, art or sports, these creative forums are full with healthy and life supporting relationships. By getting involved, through personal ascent, with places and people who are active and creative we each will develop an FAR we could enjoy.

*Following Truth brings true pleasures and brings about true Happiness*

A place or relationships are outcomes, something we reach, come to. Truth is an outcome as that which we (finally) see or realize. But is a destructive place or relationship also truth? Is coming to the end of the line, near a life threatening point, an approach to truth? By the sound and construct of these words most would say "no, that is not truth", but why not? Following the ways of FAR making R=Truth, we might discover satisfying answers. Within all sentient beings and creatures exists an inherent sense for self-preservation. If faced with imminent danger, all would seek shelter somehow, finding some way to avoid destruction. This would be an act of self-love. Feeling that we care enough about ourselves, when faced with immediate harm, our love of self surfaces and brings us to safety. The sense of self-preservation is an innate thing and mostly inanimate, being that it is awareness, an idea. Love will move us; it is a force within us all. The Universe is an ordered mechanism; it was constructed with laws and ways for its own preservation, and continuation. A planet will not suddenly, willfully go out of orbit onto a path towards its own demise, nor will a sun explode by contradicting the laws of mathematics or physics. But there are no inner conflicts within these celestial objects that we know of, which would make them act against their better interests. Love is the primary emotion; we feel this before anger or hate. No infant born hates its mother. Even wild or feral creatures can be loving and gentle towards humans when very young. A dog and a cat can be raised together as friends if introduced to each other at an early enough age. Even those two legendary enemies will be friendly and loving with one another, if hate or fear is not incurred within them.

Anger or hatred could cause someone to do that which was harmful to themselves or others. From an inner conflict, caused perhaps by rejection, a person would act in a negative and self-destructive way. But love existed first. This person would have had to have felt love in order to feel that his or her love was rejected. Their subjective and internal reason for harming themselves or others is an *isolated thing* and *not* part of Universal Truth. The emotions or conflicts that exist within them, making them behave this way, does *not* naturally exist in nature or the universe. They are not omnipresent or ubiquitous creations, they exist within specific individuals for particular and subjective reasons. Thus the outcome of these actions is not Truth.

While being aware of inherent self-preservation, those of us who act with love or self love and are drawn to or follow towards a point in the external world wherein we believe that love does or could exist then our actions are of Truth. If in an ordered and harmonious way we move towards that which we are attracted to, motivated by love, then Universal Truth is being carried out. Even if the person we are enamored of decides to reject our overture, our original act was Truth. If the individual we sought did not seek us in return perhaps an inner conflict was to blame, or the Truth of our actions went unnoticed. By acting *for* ourselves and *with* others we are doing truthful things. Others can be said to be *with us* if they either acknowledge or appreciate us. With the existence of mutual acceptance and agreement someone is then *with* another.

By creating a guide for the recognizing of Truth we would be able to feel more certain of the existence of this intangible yet centrally important thing:

*Awareness of Truth*

*Truth is/does   Truth is not*

| *Logical* | —————— | *fanciful* |
| *Understandable* | —————— | *contradictory* |
| *Helpful* | —————— | *burdensome* |

| *Positive* | —————— | *unhealthful* |
| *Freeing* | —————— | *constricting* |
| *Flow* | —————— | *cumbersome* |

| *Connect* | —————— | *isolated* |
| *Creative* | —————— | *causal* |
| *Universal* | —————— | *subjective* |

We can explore examples and illustrations of each axiom.

Truth is logical, not fanciful:

Although Truth itself rests within an ascended and eminent place, flights of fancy will not carry us there. Whereas Truth is part of an eternal order the same construct that makes Truth logical also makes it stable, lasting. It is logical to act upon self-preservation. Creating a lifestyle that includes preservation as an essential theme would necessarily be stable, as we would forgo and exclude destabilizing and unnecessary dangers. Though fanciful ideas, unrealistic whims do in a sense exist above the logical physical world they are not examples of transcendent Truth. In order for an idea, a dream or a desire to be part of or with Truth it must *not* be contrary to logic to the point where it becomes say, irrational. Admittedly certain accepted norms of logic like subjective, arbitrary inculcated mores can be too restrictive and limiting to be called Truth, still Truth itself remains logical even within its ascended position.

Truth is understandable, not contradictory:

Truth makes sense. One statement of Truth does not contradict another statement of Truth. As well Truth itself will not and does not contradict known science or reality. In order to grasp Truth it must be understood by the individual therefore it needs to be understandable and not contrived. That which is contrary to one's general learned knowledge of life is suspect, given that the knowledge has been genuinely proven even in the physical world. Truth can be communicated in an open honest way allowing it to be understood. When neither an ulterior motive nor an inner conflict is influencing words or actions the result can be Truth.

Truth is helpful, not burdensome:

It is harder and heavier to try and hide or ignore what we see as true, than it is to accept and agree with it. Truth is a guide, a light, in this way it helps us. To truly know where our home is or where food and love awaits us is a helpful thing indeed. Thus we should each embrace Truth and not attempt to run from it.

Truth is positive, not unhealthful:

As love feels good, so truth feels good. The creative and recognizable light of truth affects each of us in a positive way. Sometimes "bitter medicine" is truth. To be told, or made to face that which is important, after we have been avoiding it, can be difficult yet healthy in the long run. To keep on ignoring those issues that we would rather not see, is not a very healthful or truthful way to live.

Truth is freeing, not constricting:

The freedom experienced through truth liberates us from either dangerous or unpleasant lies. To believe a lie will keep you in an isolated place. Separate from an aspect of reality. Whatever the lie is, there is a truthful counterpart which when known will free you from the binds of a falsely constructed idea that limits your understanding. Truth naturally creates a sense of freedom that is real and secure.

Truth flows, it is not cumbersome:

When attempting to promote a lie some will often trip on their own words. To keep lies with you, within your conscious mind, will keep you from flowing naturally with life, for life itself works with truth. To be told, and to believe, untruths about life concerning that which is actually good for us, helpful really, will prevent us from working to incorporate certain beneficial aspects of reality into our lives. This vacuum, the absence of goodness, would most likely be filled by that which was not truly good as the lies about life tend to metastasize. Truth itself is of a flowing goodness, eternal and rewarding. It will flow creating happiness within us and for us unless it is blocked by obstacles caused from misunderstandings and untruths. The obstacles, however, are
temporal and can be removed through our sincere and dedicated commitment to developing, discovering truth.

Truth connects, it is not isolated:

The Truth connects us to the greater knowledge of life. Being Universal it will work with other things that we know to be true. A truth connects us to another truth and in turn brings us closer with others. An isolated idea about someone or something due to a subjective reaction or conflict will separate a person from life, if the misconception is believed to be true. Truth promotes inner Oneness as it connects the other benevolent forces that exist within us. Love, compassion, openness will each congregate with Truth creating a fullness, a wholeness for our joyful existence.

Truth is creative, not causal:

The tree is not *caused* to grow; it naturally creates the necessary things that make it ascend. The Earth is not caused to orbit a Sun that is caused to give light. These celestial events happen on their own accord without the need of an aggressive hand or force. The creativeness of Truth can be felt by our natural instinct to love, and tell the truth. An infant does not laugh when it feels the need to cry, prevarication is a learned trick and something that is caused intentionally. We are naturally drawn to that which we love, and when not being disingenuous, we will agreeably and creatively move towards that thing. The poet will create a poem, the artist will paint while the musician will express in music what he or she has come to understand and recognize as Truth.

Truth is Universal, not subjective:

That which is truth comes from an objective and ingenuous place. Subjective biases and reactions are not actual sources for truth. Something is true simply because it *is* true. It cannot be objective truth simply because someone wants it to be true, or because it serves a personal and prejudicial purpose. The purpose of truth is truth; it is its own reason for existence.

THE ELEMENTS OF HEAVEN

# *Irresistible Clarity*

The wind does not want to blow
It naturally flows
The Sun does not wish to shine
It glows
Water does not yearn to rush downhill
Unto the meadow lush
Wherein the fruits of Life await
The wetness that will nourish, sate

No hands endowed with cosmic power
Push up the night at dawn's right hour
Revealing what all know to be
The order of the days
This universal perfect system
Maintained for countless millennium
Is effortless, yet purposeful
In its workings and its ways

The way is not to want events
To turn by longing heavy will
The way of Beauty holds no secret want to fill
It is harmonious in creation
Desire does not hide or shout
In the roots of Beauty's motivation

The way itself does not hold want
None can hear the single hand
That claps in rhythm with the band
Of those who seek or are in tune
The meek the star the silent moon
The power here is not ambition
Nor vanity or controlled restriction
The way is free the limits for
Our purposes, needs
It is force majeure

KES completes an internal part of us, helping to make us whole. Following FAR reasonably and faithfully will connect us to a providing Universe. By listening to trustworthy advice within our Foundations, then Ascending with love or creativity towards beneficial and satisfying Relationships we will become harmonious and One with the Universe. Goodness recognizes goodness and rewards in measure. Though virtue might be its own reward, an unseen Universal hand lends support. For part of the genuine feeling of satisfaction we receive when being virtuous comes from a pat on the back by an acknowledging Universe. Encouraging us to continue on a well-chosen path, subtlety and silently the Universe offers its recognition and appreciation of our edifying accomplishments.

*All doors are open on the path of Truth, no barriers that we might encounter are immutable, and thus the workable steps become Choice, Flexibility then Decision*

I am not referring to or substantiating theories of alternate or hidden Universes with these comments. Whether those mostly science fiction realms exist or not I do not feel I can answer. This "New Age" has brought with it many fantastic advances in both technology and science. With these real and tangible accomplishments came many fantastic theories and ideas from dubious sources. Yet we are not speaking of everyday reality here either. Obviously, and with good reason, none can trace the source of fortuitous circumstance, or pinpoint exactly how certain good things seemed to have worked out for us. The Universe keeps its hand hidden. We might be able to trust Einstein and feel secure that those hands are not "playing dice" with our lives. But to try and understand or foresee how the cosmic matrix actually works would not be an advisable or even possible thing to do. What I am referring to is a way for people to have *faith in faith,* and afford the belief of *just rewards for just lives* a bit of science and sense. A plausible theory or answer to how and why we receive in return for our acts of benevolence. Whether or not it makes perfect *scientific* sense I cannot say. I do, however, enjoy sharing and merging the Beauty of Philosophy with the *possibilities* of Science.

Furthermore, declaring the possibility that these theorems and comforting thoughts of a responsive and benevolent Universe could be true, valid, allows each of us to remain logical even when exploring this Metaphysical realm.

With these understandings in mind we could make better choices for our lives. If the general populace had more faith and less cynicism about the value of their actions there would be more displays of generosity and tolerance in the world. By having our acts backed by tangible theories and possible results we would feel surer of our decisions. By *not* clinging to confining dogma that would force us to act or not act in certain ways, the flexibility inherent in *possibility* allows us freedom of thought.

As the R of FAR completes the formula, it also rounds off the A making our ascent more edifying. By sharing our accomplishments and growth with others in Relationships we learn even more about where we have been. It is actually unhealthy and even dangerous to seek only F&A and choosing not to include the *grounding effect* of communicating with others. The psychological results of this omission could range from haughtiness to psychosis. "The psychotic lives within the castles of the sky" constructed no doubt in isolation, and caused by too much intellectualized ascent. Those who would build these castles, but not move in, (a metaphor describing neurosis) necessarily would have developed and kept certain relationships that are grounding them. Either way A is exaggerated, out of proportion, which can be evinced by noting the anomalies of behavior. These examples of the human condition illustrate the importance of allowing ourselves to work on constructive relationships, and complete our FAR.

\* \* \*

Moreover, within the exaggerated proportions of these illusions, black or white, up or down, a person could consider themselves either: *a legend in their own minds, or a failure of the worst kind.* Neither (subjective) estimation would actually be accurate nor valid if matched up to an *objective general graph* of some sort. Hence these are each personally biased appraisals of personal worth formed by neurosis. (Though I am generally loathe citing, or validating clinical diagnoses I feel that using the term "neurosis" is helpful simply as a reference point for the reader.) Albeit not as delusional
as believing that he or she is either Superman or Bugs Bunny (which would indicate a further degradation of personality, i.e. psychosis) the neurotic idea of self can seem very convincing and correct to those experiencing such "illusory personal estimations."

\* \* \*

Along with completing the formula we would do best when constructing FAR within the parameters that it requires of us. Not unlike the non-sequential internal formation of "KSE" that we have discussed earlier, problems can be caused if we do not organize FAR wisely. Consider that the formula could be made as "FRA" if the *placement* of relationships was inappropriate within our lives. In fact that alignment, placing R *before* A is indicative of an "exaggerated ascent". For if we were to think of others as our *means to ascend* then we would place them directly next to our Foundation.

By further examining the scenario of the hasty sexual encounter described in the previous chapter we would be able to discern the presence of FRA. In understanding that both person's involved wanted to get to a better place in life quickly, they "used" each other as vehicles for Ascent. Not unlike a KSE where we would be attempting to *see happiness* in the external world, FRA reveals misinformation one would have about the process or place for ascending. An ascent is *internal* and created by that which we would personally achieve or develop within ourselves. No one can be our means for ascent we would only be causing problems for ourselves and others by attempting to make someone else our personal instrument for advancement or expansion.

In truth, this type of life malformation is similar to drug or alcohol abuse whereby an individual thinks to use something other than his or her own inner strength and creativity for internal ascent. Perhaps through an understanding of these statements we could see more of what is meant by comments like: "love is a drug", or "you've become a habit". It is not entirely outside of the realm of possibility that two people can become "addicted" to one another, attempting to use each other while causing a dependency constructed as a means to enable each to rise up to a joyous place in life. We can note also in this description an example of attempting to reach *fanciful truth* and the denial of logic. For although the best and most sincere motivations and hopes might be behind such relationships, the fact that these partnerships are formed as FRA and not FAR will usually cause them to become painful and disappointing as expectations are not realized.

*Love should be given without a price tag for one cheapens love by making it expensive*

An attachment to materialism can be seen in FRA if one equates the greatness of self with the possession of great wealth. Truly, joy is created *with* others not *from others* working *magic,* causing us to soar upwards.

The self-confidence and understanding we each will gain by looking into ourselves and learning, growing will be part of the formula for joy. As we come to realize who and what we truly are we will naturally seek to share our Inner Beauty with others, joyfully.

Thus not unlike the way in which we had discussed resolving "KSE" and creating for ourselves a healthy KES, FRA's are also solvable. If we can realize and accept the truth that following, attempting to fulfill a FRA i.e. trying to cause certain elements of the external world to somehow become our (main) sources of joy, cannot work out we would be able to forgo these futile efforts. Even while we would be disciplining ourselves, by keeping from engaging in unproductive endeavors, we would also be growing towards a more productive lifestyle, Selfhood. Indeed, I have found this type of discipline itself to be a healthy and growth promoting effort. Inner contemplation and self searching works well naturally while we are not engaged in actual physical activities. Here we afford ourselves a moment to consider our actions and the consequences of those actions. I believe that this type of inner search itself *is* an Ascent as we consciously rise to a greater understanding of ourselves and life itself. Though the physical world holds and shows us a plethora of opportunity for pleasure and pleasing events we still need to keep extrinsic possibilities in perspective. Intrinsically FRA can be transformed into joy producing FAR by holding to this paradigm. In order to actually *See* the perspective, the way in which the external world can be made to peacefully, creatively dovetail with our internal selves a KES concerning this ideal needs be developed by each of us. A perceptive outlook is required wherein the *Sight* shows us how to incorporate the physical into a delightful wholeness within us.

To be One with another is a bond not a bind. It is created from mutual and real appreciation of individual qualities and achievements. An inner Oneness develops as we learn to live more wisely and leave off making those decisions that ultimately cause complications for us. We can each grow towards Oneness using Creativity as the common denominator for both the KES and the FAR formulae. The creativeness in us can be made to serve our lives in constructive and rewarding ways. Helping us to become One within and working to create joy in our mutual environments.

*Oneness is the perfect integration of all that you are*

*Standing in the Garden*
*Is She the Ruby rose?*
*Can the Starlight see the Dreamer's wish?*
*Is Love Omnific?*
*Just suppose*

## Chapter 3

An individual would not be inspired to leave even that lonesome loft, isolated, enisled from others, or separate from an unhealthy relationship to become part of the "general malaise of society". Thus why not unearth, discover a truly plentiful place, already created. The essence of Life *cannot* be simply a "normal world" full with hypocrisy and contradiction, where survival is the greatest goal and happiness is merely the whim of imaginative poets. One needs to, for but an instant, consider an infinite Universe that grows more mysterious even as science grows more knowledgeable, to be able to catch a glimpse of essential existence rich with gratifying pleasures and joy.

As we begin this third chapter the ideal of finding the right place and people for fulfillment is introduced. By seeking a *fuller height* rather than a different emptiness the dualistic and inefficacious "problem and solution" cure is avoided. We should not simply address the symptoms and leave the actual malady untreated. Boredom, discontentment or discomforts are too unattractive to be able to draw individuals out of isolation. One would have need of a more appealing enticement in order to be motivated to leave the comfort zone of an imagined solitude. It does exist, this place of natural beauty that so many have yearned for and written of. It exists exactly where the normal world does not. Not that this place is abnormal nor would it require any degree of lunacy to be a member of this earthly wonder, to the exact contrary, one needs to be natural and whole him or herself. I make the statement that: *there is no such thing as normal* for entwined within the wild world of murder, mayhem and mundanity there are three opposing and non-conciliatory aspects. They exist as: normal-abnormal-unnatural each contradicting and unappeased by the others.

Mostly it is called normal because the majority lives there and has survived incredible and innumerous attempts at its demise. The normal or "real world" is filled with survivors who daily and moment-by-moment deal with the incongruity of a normal-abnormal-unnatural situation. The word normal is merely a barometric indication letting society know that things remain at the status quo. But the barometer of one society can read totally differently from that of another. The status quo in America reads as (mainly) peaceful and (mostly) prosperous if this were true of the whole world, I probably wouldn't be writing this book. As it is, the readings in many countries around the globe tell the "baro-masters", to coin a phrase, that the populace in well under control, not too many are starving and human rights are not being spoken of too loudly.

Here, in the U.S. abnormalities become publicly known via the prime time news when a normal reporter tells us about some horrific event or a socially abnormal deed that has taken place. When the stress of this cyclical and demanding situation gets to be too much the abnormal or unnatural parts start being loosed from their normal controls and life becomes, or seems to become dangerous. It is unnatural, essentially, for living sentient beings to purposely hurt themselves, or harm others in a premeditated and willful fashion. Yet all this does exist and has existed beginning probably even before man began recording history. One might suppose that the answer to these three opposing forces, normal-abnormal-unnatural, would be three harmonious or balanced ones, or maybe more than three would be needed to offset the amount of energy the inward conflict involves. But in truth it requires only one. We can leave the place of irreconcilable and circular normal-abnormal-unnatural by becoming simply Natural *within,* working *with* the Universe. Not normal, for there is no such quality in actual life, but naturalness exists in abundance.

\* \* \*

By way of further explanation one could consider that the "term" normal is indicative of an *arbitrary point of view* that indeed changes in import and importance depending on where one is in the world. Differently, Naturalness is a definitive and established aspect of Life. A Natural *thing* like an apple or orange has the same construct no matter where on Earth one is. Except for indigenous varieties and say, soil or climate conditions each Natural thing is approximately exactly the same all over Earth. Not so with "normal". What would be considered normal to a society of cannibalistic jungle dwellers is stuff that film noir provides for the western world moviegoers' astonishment. Basically normal defines the *status quo* of a majorities opinions in a given state or region. Contrastingly, Natural is more like a state of innocence purged and free from societies cerebral (and often unhealthful) influence.

To return "back to Nature" would necessitate leaving a "manmade arbitrary existence" and allow our *individual roots* to be our main source for growth and sustenance.

\* \* \*

As we within begin to resolve and leave the lonely, disunited normal world of discontentment and begin our journey towards Naturalness, the external, the Earth around us, will begin to appear more natural, peaceful and joyful. With a lessening of duality and opposing forces going on in one's mind and essence the actual reality of life will become more evident, perceivable. We will be able to See, notice, and appreciate the real beauty of existence transcendent above the cacophony of illusion. As the normal world thankfully begins to fade, our Natural selves will start to appear and an appreciation of life will arise. There is delicateness within this Natural order, even though it is essentially much greater and more powerful than normal life. This earthly land requests that each who would enter and reside within it become less dualistic and more One with its beauty. Better balance and harmony is needed to avoid being the veritable "bull in the china shop", therefore we would need an Internal *with* External way for existence.

A common and disconcerting dualism too often occurs mentally, in life, as one intends to be, believes in, being benevolent, gracious and magnanimous but acts contrary to those ideals. We might promise others or ourselves that we will (always) be that wonderful person that we have shown ourselves to be, and then sometime afterwards act contradictory to our pledge. Words themselves, in essence, are products of the intellect; they are inanimate incorporeal, as thoughts are. Deeds are physical actions that take place in the corporeal world. Here, in *the cerebral space* between *Words (or thoughts) and Deeds* lies the crux of the duality. Here is where a "common denominator" is needed. We require, in order to bring together, into Oneness, our Thoughts with our

Actions a balancer and/or a harmonizing agent. We would each profit by having, developing a creative yet potent force that we could rely upon and entrust with this most beneficent and important role. We need inner Love.

Love is the one force that can guide both our cognitive and physical activities, decisions. It can work as the balancing factor for thoughts and the synchronizer of actions. These insights lead us to the third formula:

$$\frac{C}{L} \cong \frac{D}{L}$$ or: *Contemplate Love congruent with Doing Love.*

As C=Contemplate, D=Do, or Doing and L=Love. Contemplate love congruently with doing love, this can work out for each of us. Love is the first cousin of creativity, which makes this internal force the perfect source for balanced and pleasant contemplation. Love is powerful enough to stimulate our thoughts while inspirationally motivate us towards positive actions. We might start this formula for meditation in a premeditative way, by consciously and purposely considering love then acting accordingly. If we continue with this type of inward working, allowing our love and our belief in love, to guide us, after a while it can become as second nature, completely natural. Love is a strong enough force to be able to deal with conflict or mundanity. With the former, love can mitigate internal or external disharmony, in the latter love can stimulate and inspire us to each beyond the ennui that can exist in day-to-day life. Ultimately, it requires less energy, and is more natural, to follow through, in our actions, with thoughts influenced or stimulated by love than it is to act negatively on an angry impulse or reaction. Consider that most of us tell ourselves to "hold on" before lashing out or overtly expressing our anger, even when it is justified. But when we feel a loving impulse or inspiration we *encourage* ourselves to express it. This would indicate that there is a natural flow within us to go with love, a course that begins with thought and inspiration completing itself with words or actions. These insights indicate that **C/L** $\cong$ **D/L** is a natural and genuine way of being.

As we study the use of " $\cong$ " or congruency as the merging ratio the question "why not use + or *and*" as the connector might arise. But a "+" or "plus" would indicate that we should *always* act with love, similarly "and" would urge us to do love at all times. I believe that this would be asking too much of ourselves while being basically unhealthful. For indeed to require, obligate us to always love is tantamount to being controlled by love; it would negate the relevancy of just anger and compromise love's commitment to freedom. With the use of " $\cong$ " the idea of congruency or balance is established. By acting congruently with our thoughts we are doing that which our insight, acumen foresees. So that none might confuse the advocating of **C/L** $\cong$ **D/L** with an overall and universal exhortation to love, or for all to love everyone, the understanding of this formula's Natural and Universal properties is essentially needed.

For us to use love, our love, as an ambassador an ombudsman for our thoughts is different basically than contemplating love itself. Using love as the mitigator, the balancer of even angry or frustrating mental moments *congruent* with actions, or words (for I hold that Words characteristically *are* Deeds as they are heard or noted by others in the physical world), is a description of a natural and harmonious way of being. If one does not feel that much love towards the situation, then they would act with as much love as they feel is necessary or right according to their own self examined belief of love. However, the formula does encourage us to act with love, if this is what is inspiring us. To amiably reply to that passerby who said "hello" in a genuine and open manner without feeling abashed about an honest and spontaneous display of emotion. We can also learn to be able to hold back from spontaneous vexation, like throwing apples at our misunderstood neighbor, while we discover the true nature of the situation.

*One need never feel foolish when being sincere*

If indeed these instances describe, illustrate a more natural way of being, and I do espouse this as such, then they could be seen as ready examples and keys for getting out of the "normal cycle" and into naturalness. By applying some Darwinian logic to Spiritual evolution we might be able to see some empirical, practical and observable workings and ways of the formula $C/L \cong D/L$. For if we begin by first consciously, meditatively working on this natural method, then continuing our development by acting upon, behaving with ways of love, the creative process itself will become second nature as we grow towards *unconsciously* carrying out our beliefs of love. Furthermore, that which was normal but unhealthy, hence: unnecessary, would disappear, be transcended. Not unlike the theory of "evolutionary adaptation" wherein a living thing is seen to either lose or gain certain characteristics, depending on their usefulness, we would evolve naturally and Spiritually by behaving as such. Specific normal traits of living that are not essentially healthful, (therefore not essential) like acting on angry impulses or feeling forced to show love, would begin to vanish as we began to act and live more in touch with our true natures. This theory of evolution applied to Spirituality and Naturalness is logical and viable. For if we began and then continued to work with ourselves in a natural manner, for harmonious and natural outcomes, our relationships and our lives in general will evolve to greater happiness and comfort.

By borrowing from the treatise of "natural selection" within the well known and discussed *Evolutionary Theory* and restating the belief that the natural aspects of life exist as our latent and potent inner strengths, we can lend even greater validity to the promise of becoming fuller individuals in a more beautiful environment. As the normal and unnecessary aspects of life begin to fade, along with their more hazardous abnormal and unnatural cohorts we will evolve out of a confusing personal plurality and into Oneness. Oneness encompasses all that we (truly) are; this is not to be confused with many, multiple or conflicting personalities. Each aspect of our natural selves can work with each other one. Thus the artist in us could work either in the kitchen or the garden creating colorful banquets or bouquets. The mathematician could be useful in summing up people, situations or household income, figuring net worth. The athlete could appear at work or play as we develop our natural physical skills for different uses. As we merge our inner artistry with calculated understanding of life and self, we will discover innumerable choices and chances for rewards. Thus Oneness is an inward harmony, a collective that welcomes and nourishes all of our innate abilities and personae. Different, and infinitely more gratifying than normal, where we would all be similar, like the next guy in the same boat, we can evolve to a natural yet unique spirituality. We each could realize Oneness, being in harmony within, with others and with our Earth.

The practicality of learning through "opposites", like yin and yan, becomes apparent in certain metaphysical discourses such as the one we are currently engaged in. Thus in order to better describe and explain what the esoteric state of Oneness is like; we could more readily discuss exactly what it is not like. It is not aggressive, yet it is *not* ineffective. It is not normal, yet it is not "supernatural", or illusory. It is in no way unpleasant, yet one will remain free from euphoric delusions or visions of grandiosity within true Oneness. To paraphrase a noted economist I can state that: The world is manic-depressive, sometimes. Ups and downs, and high ups and low downs, are typical in the dualistic arena of the normal world. But even more ephemeral and impossible to actually locate than the concept of "society", where exactly *is* this real world? We can all see Nature clearly; we would even see the tree fall in the forest if we were standing close enough to it. But if you were asked to point out the location of the real or normal world, where would you direct your finger? It might sound platitudinal at worst and ironic obviously, but perhaps the Truth is that: the "real world" is the illusion.

In reality that idea is not all that new for a noteworthy 17th century French essayist once remarked that: "The exact contrary of what is generally believed is often the truth". There have been historic and recorded glimpses into essential truth throughout the ages, but it is up to each of us to follow those ideas to where they can lead. Philosophers, poets and prophets have each revealed and shared their deepest insights, revelations and epiphanies. Their works include the essays that humanity has held in respect and reverence. The timeless poets' metered verses illustrate and elucidate the beauty of the Natural world thereby exhorting all to seek. The mystical and mysterious prophets have, throughout the ages, revealingly described "other realms" blessed with beatific peace.

*　*　*

Not unlike Plato's cave wherein the inhabitants mistake shadows for real entities the "catchword" *real world* has been somehow upgraded to a *given*. Furthermore, why is it that one "faces reality" when he or she admits to something negative or disturbing? Why cannot one "see the real" as it is: bountiful and beautiful *but* infringed upon and distressed by "normal events".

*　*　*

Words and written thoughts are our external maps to all manner of internal realities. Whether or not we choose to explore where and what these maps are indicating and leading to is entirely up to us.

*One would be using limited sight when seeing the forest without perceiving a system in its roots*

The formula **C/L** $\cong$ **D/L** differs slightly in conception from the other formulae in as much as it would be something we would choose to adopt, rather than it being a constant in nature. Although I have indeed chosen to use and incorporate this paragon and meditative practice within my own life, I do not believe that I am either the only individual who does, or the first one to do so. I am certain that many thoughtful, philosophical and good people have adopted these ideas. Perhaps not in an entirely conscious or describable way, they have learned to incorporate the harmony of love with balanced equations about life within their respective lives. From these observations we can deduce that the formula *lends itself* to human nature rather than being a created part of it. It can be learned and used for our benefit if we choose to do so.

The effectiveness, accord and potential power that rest within the formula's construct and application could be brought out through this proverb:

*Power without the unifying influence of Love is destructive*
*Love without the reckoning force of Power is ineffective.*
*However, Love merged harmoniously with Power is*
*perfection enough to guide History's course*

\* \* \*

The word, idea or reality of "power" should not be confused with (physical) ability, and especially not "negative ability". To gain spiritual power an individual needs to have passed many tests and learned much about life and his or herself. The power to help create happiness and joy in the world is a principle magnanimous goal of benevolence. This potency is conferred on those who have incorporated the properties of love within their everyday existence. The charismatic philanthropist has earned it, as has the eastern Guru and erudite scholar. Each is able to help others through their loving understanding of Self.

All this being said (about Spiritual power) there does exist, in the corporeal and corporate world a measure of *materialistic power* that can be obtained through the accumulation of wealth and/or position. There are, of course, numerous (or perhaps unfortunately *innumerous)* documented cases where power itself has "corrupted" certain persons. The temptation to *override Nature's laws* and forcibly *control outcomes* by using, or misusing, power is a lamentable example of human proclivity. However, in accord with the above aphorism and the "Principles for Laws" discussed in chapter 1

the initiating of *philosophy over psychology* would be a sufficient discipline for allowing "Spiritual Power (internal)" to oversee and guide psychical "power" or (external)ability and disallow malfeasance and malice of wealth.

\* \* \*

If we Contemplate love then we are not "taking away" from others, consciously. We are not looking down on our fellow man or woman or finding some subjective and biased flaw in them. To Contemplate love and *not* take away, from others, would be a main goal in working with the formula. Too often a portion of the general population walks through life, thinking negatively towards those they see or know, mentally engaging in the taking away, the detracting from others. How much of a days precious hours are spent by prejudicially summing up another's shortcomings and differences when each of us could be developing a more beautiful and insightful lifestyle? This type of cognitive behavior is contrary to the point and purpose of **C/L** ≅ **D/L** and can only lead to negative or hurtful actions. The "ability" to take away from people in one's mind is a base and physical thing, neither essential nor praiseworthy; it is an unfortunate trait of some who live in the normal world. Usually accepted and an occasion for ridicule or derisive laughter these negative ideas are shared between comrades in normal circumstances. We need not go too far into the social abyss of late night comedy, tabloid mentality or yellow journalism, for instance, to be able to recognize the problem there, and be unmotivated to spread negative gossip.

This type of conscious behavior is a learned thing, and as such it can be unlearned. We can work with ourselves and avoid negative thinking towards others, judgments about everyday people that have neither basis in goodness or even reality. By letting go of that which is consciously unpleasant and unnecessary, our actions and our lives will benefit. I cannot see a good mood, or true happiness being created by adding to one's mind that which they have taken away from another and mentally making themselves seem superior. That type of mathematic calculation is not something one could construct a good life from.

As we begin to form more positive conclusions about people, learn and accept the reality of our Sameness and appreciate our individual differences, the Benevolent Universe will only reward our efforts. The Cosmos being transcendent beyond pettiness, and containing all manner of pleasantries for us, would be a wonderful and welcomed inclusion for our lives. In order to accurately and realistically incorporate Universal forces into a formula we would need to consider certain suppositions. If we *could* consider or believe that there is and would be a positive response to us, if and when we acted benevolently then this could be one of the Theorems. We might, as we had discussed earlier, be able to believe or hope that there would be a measured and certain reaction from an encompassing Universe, rewarding us and supporting our efforts. A continuation from forces we cannot really see that would complete the formula making it whole, as:

$$\frac{C}{L} \cong \frac{D}{L} \blacktriangle Re=L$$

or:

*Contemplate Love congruent with Doing Love,*
therefore *Receive Love*

As the symbol: "▲" would represent "therefore" and Re: receive. We might not be able to determine where these "gifts of love" would come from exactly, but we can begin to define what they would be. A gift of love could be just that, meeting the right person at the right time as the Universe brings you together with your true love to be. As *Love brings love* our ways of working with unseen forces could bring us untold largesse even in the form of romantic togetherness. Monetary benefits could also be part of what we would be receiving for there is nothing *intrinsically* wrong with having money. The ways in which we acquire and use financial wealth will determine whether it is essentially bounty or booty. To gain a financial lift from the Cosmos as stipend for our good deeds is perfectly sound and honest. Then to use it wisely and share some of this natural wealth with others could be descriptive of an advanced civilization that has developed some excellent meditative skills.

Psychology has dealt much with the concept of "archetypes" since the early 20th century.

Although the number of archetypes is basically limitless, they each are representative of a certain *type of individual* and are of themselves *singular.*

Some examples of notable archetypal images are:

The *Child*
The *Hero*
The *Great Mother*
The *Wise old man*
The *Trickster*

Each and all of these become acknowledged by our unconscious minds. I have come to, however, recognize certain identifications mostly made by our *preconscious* minds that I have termed "macrotypes". I believe that we identify the "world" as male:father and "society" as female:mother. The "world-father" is more immovable, monolithic and larger than "society-mother". He holds many physical gifts for us in his buildings (that "she" can provide) i.e. the world's department stores, automobile outlets, etc. and is an authority (figure) in our lives. Maintaining sometimes arbitrary and intractable rules we must follow either at work or in day-to-day life. He can be hard to connect with, stubborn at times, but we seek to be on good terms with him. I believe that many people's worldview is influenced by their relationship with their actual fathers. Those who are "angry at the world" probably have some unresolved animosity towards their childhood fathers. Those who blame the world for their problems might in fact be blaming their fathers for their current troubles. Individuals who have resolved childhood difficulties, or had good relationships with their fathers in their youth would be more likely to function ably in the world-father domain. Our "society-mother" inculcates certain mores and ways of behavior for us to follow. She can also bequeath upon us our tastes in fashion and palate unless we are still rebelling against her as our actual mother. We could be talkative in social settings like she was, or taciturn or gregarious depending on what aspects of her personality we can most easily adopt and identify with. Furthermore, if we are good to her, act well and do well in society, then world-father will let her provide many good things for us to enjoy. Each of us might be able to discern or discover the reason for a number of our personality traits by reexamining our relationship with our parents, or the male and female guardians that we were raised by. Ideas of liberalness or conservativeness, openness or intolerance towards others in society-world could each be counterparts of parental influence.

Modern psychology defines "self-actualization" as the state where a person realizes their greatest potential. In eastern thought, the "atman" is our true self, the essence of what and who we really are, universally. What I believe is missing in these two relevant and real teachings are viable and natural methods of getting there and actualizing our Self.

Also many eastern ideas include calls for asceticism and self-denial, which I believe are mainly unnecessary and can even be dangerous. Western psychology includes an understanding of the value in receiving personal pleasures and rewards, but has failed to recognize the Universe's part in this. A western scholar is quoted as saying "philosophy is psychology without application". But psychology is mostly application without a sound or universal philosophy for life.

In chapter one I had introduced the term psychespirituality wherein mind and spirit work toward a common goal. Self-actualization as it is defined today does not, I believe, include the progress to a spiritual evolution. That is, the growth of an individual from, for instance, a dependant person to someone independent and more in control of his or her destiny is charted, but the development of Spirituality is not included. Following is a diagram whereby we might see a conscious and emotional progress that develops to the point of certain Spiritual ideologies and personal understandings:

**Evolution of the Individual**
within pychespirituality

**Unhealthy**
dependant, feelings of inadequacy

**Socially accepted**
independent, controlling, inward conflicts

**Spiritually developed**
inner-oneness, individual integration

**Unhealthy**
displaced anger

**Socially accepted**
justifiably angry but lashing out at others

**Spiritually developed**
peaceful, focused, honest with self

**Unhealthy**
isolated from the external and others

**Socially accepted**
in the status quo functioning normally

**Spiritually developed**
self-aware, flowing/working with the external

With these formulae for life and the philosophies that accompany them I have attempted to bridge the schism that exists between east and west. Also by explaining the ideas with nature and universe in mind, the psychology goes hand in hand with philosophical applications. These applications are meant to be applied in the "here and now" thus avoiding distant theories and the somewhat intangible mystical promises for future rewards. By a fuller understanding of our lives and ourselves I believe we can each find rewarding satisfaction in the present.

For instance, with further investigation into my comments: "if we are good to her, act well and do well in society, then world-father will let her provide many good things for us to enjoy" we might be able to unravel some mysteries of behavior and outcomes. How many of us are affected by this ping-pong way of living, or how deeply? Believing that we will be rewarded "someday" by working with world-father diligently we await the gifts that society-mother will bestow on us. In reality society *does* hold much delightful and luxurious bounty, but that fact can make the duality seem more real. We could be thinking or hoping that we will someday receive some of the rewards we see in department stores, luxury automobile dealerships and wealthy neighborhoods. These tangible possibilities could be keeping us in the "ping-pong match" as we bounce back and forth between world-father and society-mother. Many of us will have a dispiriting experience when or if disappointment occurs. Some would even feel crushed, as this future promise does not materialize. Yet if we were to observe this outcome by examining the reality of macrotypes it would make actual sense. Of course we would be disappointed by a "non-entity" society-mother is not real; she does not faithfully follow a benevolent course rewarding us for our efforts. She does not really exist. Neither does world-father whose word we trusted when he told us that honest work would bring rewards. He too is a projected manifestation of our preconscious minds. We can only wonder how much these psychological apparitions affect an individual's belief in God.

Through personal meditations we will discover that macrotypes are not the omega, the end all and be all óf life. Beyond these "almost tangible" manifestations exist actual forces and truths that are benevolent and can provide for us. This is something that I firmly believe and have personally seen and experienced in my own life. The realities that rest a few steps past our visions of macrotypes are perhaps the trusted truths that we have been seeking all along. We might have gotten distracted or misdirected when the non-entities began to affect us. We went looking to receive instant gratification from a plethora of social offerings, or we stopped, waiting for our just rewards. There is still time and opportunity to get back to our original focus and hopes.

The Universal provider is not as easy to recognize or identify as is our individual parents cum macrotypes who we have known so well. Without entering into a theological discourse, but letting our minds look past and a bit beyond society-world I wonder how distant these forces really are. It is possible to become aware, through personal introspection, of having an actual *direct relationship* with macrotypes. We would be able to see if we were relating to the world at large and society in general as if they were our father and mother. If this does exist within us then how difficult, and how rewarding, would it be to develop a positive relationship with more influential and resourceful providers who are not restrained by mortal limitations? Perhaps some would be able to resolve unsettled issues about their parents or the world itself by working with this greater provider. By meditating on the formula $C/L \cong D/L \blacktriangle Re=L$ and looking past the normal world and social boundaries we can help ourselves to evolve as spiritual individuals.

* * *

It would not really require a Herculean effort to reach the summit of Mt. Selfhood using our inward strength and resolve in order to ascend. Nor would it be a Sisyphean task, overworking for many years but never coming to fruition and satisfaction. What could be the outcome, the benevolent, expansive development we might reach by incorporating our True Natures with our Spirits for lasting accomplishments? Consider the beauty, the rewards!

Veritably, these achievements would require us to use, incorporate our True Natures and Spirits for their (our) Realization. Hence this understanding indicates firstly, that we need to actually develop, evolve towards our real natures and spiritual strengths. Secondly, we need to purge and/or transcend negative based ability and effort like those displays of displaced anger and such. For how much, and at what cost to life do the self-defeating and destructive acts and energies add up to, or more to the point, subtract from us?

Not unlike the ways in which we discussed changing a KSE or a FRA into their more natural and beneficial counterparts, similar types of meditative disciplines could work for the developmental change to natural and (more) spiritual growth. One of modern psychology's axioms with which I very much agree states: "you are not responsible for what you feel, but you are responsible for what you do". By acknowledging the wisdom in this statement and using it as a guide for behavior we can allow ourselves certain reactions and responses to life but still hold off from acting on those reactions. For instance, as we have learned from previous chapters in this work about the useful and beneficial prescience and self-control called upon as we nurture and change a KSE to a KES (and FRA to FAR) we can also change and nurture our actions and reactions to various stimuli. If as we travel the path of self-realization, actualization we find ourselves reacting in an unspiritual or aggressive way we can still hold off from actually acting on those responses. Being responsible for what we do by keeping from physical and/or verbal displays of contentiousness while we "dig deeper" into our selves reaching for that fount of love and creativity, we will grow and develop spiritually.

This type of natural discipline can be extremely beneficial

and ultimately strengthening and helpful. If we continue with this: holding off externally as we grow internally, eventually the actual reactions will dissipate even disappear replaced by inward self-confidence and creative peace. In this way we can guide and work with ourselves for self-love and peaceful coexistence with others.

\* \* \*

THE ELEMENTS OF HEAVEN

# *Venus in Paradise*

The magic of the morn is pure
The loving sun shines softly
It lets the earth feel warm and sure
With its yellow harmony

The sky accepts the cloud's intrusion
The trees are green with joy
There is no jealousy or illusion
No devices to employ

Resolutions rest in Truthfulness
Spared from sacrifice
Freedom reigns with creativeness
For Venus in paradise

She may be seen as love incarnate
Or loves unending message
Sweet in strength, ever animate
Beauty claims her visage

There is the peace of acquiescence
No word is mentioned twice
The listener hears the meaning's essence
My bride thrives in paradise

While bearing in mind ways of behavior and relating with others in society consider that:

*Spiritual Virtue need not be sacrificial*

Virtue itself is goodness' strength; it is the active part of standard and stationary Goodness. Thus how we act, what we actually do can be considered either virtuous or not. As virtue is strength and strength is ability we can use our potential wisely or unjustly depending on which we happen to choose given an opportunity. Here the subject becomes *advantage* and how we would use a natural or circumstantial advantage. Those who are physically stronger than others have a corporal advantage in certain social or public arenas. Those who are wealthier have a material advantage in life. These endowments could be used or misused depending on an individual's awareness of or adherence to the ideals of virtue.

With contemplation of this aphorism:

**Virtue states:**
*Never misuse advantage*
*But always use advantage*
*Never loose(sight of)advantage*

We can examine these ideas:

A farmer has a large crop of corn and owns many acres of land in a mostly impoverished village. His neighbors range from unemployed and malnourished inhabitants to poor farmers with small crops. The fact that he has much affords him the flexibility of choice and possibilities. His decisions could be based on how he views Virtue, to what extent he believes that this is an important or relevant aspect of life. As well his understanding of the *ways of Virtue* will guide his decision process. Following are several scenarios that could arise from this situation:

Having little care for anyone outside his own family, and feeling that Virtue is for saints and martyrs he discards his extra food and does not help his neighbors at all.

He is a misanthropist and works to rid himself of his poor neighbors and their land by forcing them off their property. He uses his wealth to gain more wealth and laughs derisively at the idea of Virtue.

Discovering that he has trouble sleeping because of thoughts and dreams about the unfortunate people of his village, he decides to act with Virtue. By utilizing his advantage of having extra food, he decides to give most of his surplus to the villagers.

They praise him and adore his efforts so he sleeps well as is kind to his own family. But one season does not bring as much food; he did not foresee this possibility. He had lost sight of an event that happened some years past when the harvest was scant. Thus for one year he loses the advantage of extra food, and the villagers get angry because of their lack of sustenance.

He vows that this dearth of produce will never occur again, in learning that

*Wisdom keeps the currency of Virtue strong* he gives seeds to his neighbors helping them to increase their own yield. He also allows some of his burden to ease by hiring helpers for his farm and paying them mostly with food and shelter. The extra hands present him the possibility of expanding the size of his own crop. Thus the new season brings with it more food, good friends and further wealth. By not misusing his advantage he sleeps well and enjoys self-love. By wisely using the advantage of having more than others the whole village prospers and life is better for all involved. By keeping in sight the reality that he cannot control certain forces in his life, such as Nature's vagaries, he protects his future by making sure he has sufficient food in surplus.

By incorporating his own understanding with a formula for life he has helped himself, and others, create a delightful existence. He engaged the ways and means available to him constructively and creatively improving his world and securing his future.

## *I Am*

I am King David dodging the greedy Goliaths
Darting in between
The crashing thrashing monoliths
I am keeping the Philistines at bay
Warding the Leviathan away
Working with magic and ironsmiths

I am Santiago sailing on a violent sea
Flowing with the typhoon
No untoward waves come from me
I am keeping the predators at bay
Warding the craggy bottom away
Bringing home my precious bounty

I am Ulysses I will not heed a siren's song
I am on an ancient quest
Whereby right shall conquer wrong
I am keeping the hags at bay
Warding the curses away
Within my new Eden do I belong

I am Don Quixote jousting against illusion
That is not mine for me reality
Has risen above confusion
I am keeping cliché's at bay
Warding the critics away
Riding my words like a stallion

I am Humanity struggling to survive
By wit and grit and fortune's benefit
I manage to stay alive
I am keeping the cynics at bay
Warding dystopia away
Being my own poet, promise, prophet

*If I were in the forest*
*Where the way went west or east*
*I believe that I would choose that path*
*Which resisted me the least*

# Chapter 4

With the creation and establishment of a unifying formula which itself evolves to incorporate a Benevolent Universe, we can focus mainly on the exterior world. Having successfully and harmoniously merged our Internal realities with the external, we can now work towards some of the more elusive but edifying solutions in life. As we look out over our immediate environment what are some of the ideas and motives present in our eyes and minds? Are we searching for what we can easily or safely take from life? Do we focus mainly on the possibilities or the obstacles that exist before us? In what way do we search, what is the central theme or drive within us which in itself can determine the outcomes and energies involved in our quests. If we are trying to cause an event, make certain things go our way, then the energy will be aggressive and could be inharmonic. But as we peer out over the horizon calling on and in touch with the wealth and power of Creativity within us, possibilities become apparent and not too distant.

As we stand within ourselves gazing at the panorama before us, we can wonder about how much of life itself we have rejected. Perhaps a number of events that we had tried to cause did not go our way. Maybe they backfired making us look foolishly human. Frustrated, annoyed or angry we decided to withdraw from the scene, we walked away petulantly, then into ourselves where we stand somewhat removed from life. Some might have felt so angry and misunderstood that now they use this place apart from others as a vantage point. Safely removed from the central arena, guarded in a fortress within them, they decide to take back whatever they can from life and people. Blaming an unfair world for their troubles, they feel justified in carrying out furtive or aggressive acts against others. Opportunity will make a thief out of those who are looking to get even or ahead. But whatever pelf might be taken from existence, can it be truly satisfying, rewarding or lasting?

If we have acted this way, finding a means for revenge or recompense we might have re-examined our actions as dissatisfaction or remorse set in after realizing that those who we had taken from have most likely had quite similar experiences as we. They too had been foiled in some grand scheme, and are as frustrated as we about life in general. Perhaps, after understanding their fate a bit more, we decide to adopt the proverb "honor amongst thieves" and leave off stealing a piece of life from another.

Discovering, in essence, that this type of behavior does not work, as it bothers our humane conscience and fails to fulfill our dreams, we would look for an alternative way to be.

*There exists an internal fundamental difference between ambition and a dream. Moreover, this distinction defines and categorizes both endeavors making them either a basically selfish goal or a magnanimous purpose. The ambitious person selfishly works to prove something or other, whereas the dreamer optimistically seeks to share things with others*

If we honestly and with good purpose looked over the events and circumstances that caused us to fail, we might be able to discover the actual reasons and redress them. But first we might need to define "failure". We could have come to understand that it was the idea of failure that caused us to reject the world, but what exactly did we fail in? If the orange grower thought that he was planting apples and wound up growing the citrus fruit instead, did he fail? If someone dreamed, or fantasized about building a castle on a mountaintop and then slipped on a stone while on their way up, would they consider this to be failure? We did not fail if what we were attempting to do was, in reality, impossible to accomplish in the first place. If we misunderstood certain laws of Nature then the outcome from our ignorance was not a loss, it was a lesson.

*If you seek to climb a mountain, begin not by digging a hole*

None can cause the rain to start or stop by shouting at the sky. That actuality is most obvious. But what are some of the lesser-known things that we try to cause? Are there still events and circumstances we wish to control, or feel perturbed at the fact that we were unable to see our desires done? Once we have gotten past what does not work, because of Natural limitations or contrariness to established and necessary laws in life, we can explore rational and reasonable alternatives.

While in contact with our inner creativeness we can look for ways and means to fulfill our dreams for the wholeness of our lives. Creatively, without taking away, we can incorporate available means for success and achieve whatever is actually possible. These ideas bring us to the final formula presented in this writing:

$$Sce \cong W+M[\}Li$$

or Self creative congruent with Ways and Means for Life. As Sce=Self creative, is congruent with, W=Ways, M=Means, "[}" represents the idea of "for" or "serving what purpose", Li=Life.

There are a number of essential aspects of life needed in order to complete wholeness. If we omit or reject that which we should include in our lives we cannot hope to reach actual fulfillment. There are eight essential amino acids necessary for building healthy and hale bodies. If we fail to consume the required amount of protein we will not see our potential. We could be eating well, exercising and getting a sufficient amount of rest but if we omitted vitamin C from our diet entirely disease would set in.

By describing and examining some prerequisites for life we can focus our abilities towards positive directions. Deciding that we have developed creatively, and hold that potential within us, and with us, we can connect congruently to various ways for fulfillment. Ways in life are the openings or possibilities we see. Beginning from a desire or dream within our Self-creativeness, we seek a way to fulfill our important ideas.

We could be searching our memories, our present or our presently situated place in order to find a way for satisfaction. Trying to remember what roads we took that led us to that great restaurant while we are driving and hungry. We then switch gears to the present as we see a sign that looks familiar. The sign is situated in front of a fork in the road; we are presented with the choice of going one way or another. Finally we recognize that tree along the side of the road that stands two blocks from our desired destination; we decide to follow this path.

The *way* we have seen and chosen leads us to the *means* for satisfying our hunger, our desire to be fed. The restaurant rises up like some desert oasis and we complete this single path for life by entering through the door. Once seated, and with the menu before us, we again begin the process of **Sce** ≅ **W+M[}Li** by looking into ourselves trying to determine what exactly we are in the mood for, what do we want to eat. Again there are different choices and we search this menu looking for the way that will bring us to the means of fulfillment. There under "entrees" we could find the means, steak, potatoes and a salad will do very nicely for our need of self-preservation i.e. food.

People too, can be, or become means for us. Sharing happiness or reaching a desired point in life often necessitates the inclusion of others in our plans. The owner of the store we work in or the CEO of our place of employment can each become a means for our advancement. The attractive secretary or personable co-worker could become our means for sharing our joy of life.

While considering the ways in which we could incorporate these individuals with our desired outcomes, we might be reminded of how we got to this place originally. Back when we were seeking employment how did we approach those who we now are familiar with? If we are on good grounds with them we might seek their assistance now in helping us to ascend even higher, to a raise in salary or perhaps a more intimate relationship.

On considering the nexus "$\cong$" which connects our inner creativity with a *way that we see* we can affirm that we have avoided various problems which could and do exist in life. By working to be *congruent* with the External world, which has and holds countless ways and means for our fulfillment, we will keep clear of being: *possessive, aggressive* and *over-demanding* or controlling. Those types of personality traits would determine that a person's relationship with his or her environments was inharmonious, not actually balanced and most likely unsatisfying. Understandably and within the blueprint of Natural Laws people and/or places cannot be our *foundation* for happiness, we need to build and create that fundamental ourselves, but others can help us to reach personal and mutual fulfillment. Thus by definition and reality, Happiness is something we would experience within us while Fulfillment would be that which we See in and receive from the world around us.

By working within our environments in a creative harmonious way we could incorporate various means for life's fullness and plentitude. The formula **Sce $\cong$ W+M[}Li** begins within our mutual selves, connecting to our conscious vision for seeing ways for us to communicate or express our individual dreams or desires in the physical world. Continuing towards completion, the process advocates working towards those goals by advancing for life, our lives. Whereas **C/L $\cong$ D/L** provides a method for accordant living within the External, **Sce** ≅ **W+M[}Li** leads directly *into the External* where we can realize life's fullness.

Through the inner connectivity of "≅", congruency, we would be using our Sight, or intellect, in balance and harmony as we search the External world. Rather than acting on an aggressive or destructive desire that would take away from a physical means and do that which was against life, the formula explains a complete and realistic approach for our dreams. If we were to, for the sake of teaching by opposites, draw up or illustrate the formula *conversely*, it might look and sound as: "aggressively seeing a W-M X li, or aggressively seeing a way to take away from means against life".

As *means* exist in the physical world and can be, touched, seen, smelled, heard, hence: sensed by our senses, our relationship with them can be either "+" or "-," plus or minus. If we begin, within ourselves, creatively, connecting to Sight or Mind congruently the natural impetus will be "W+M", as we poised and appropriately find a positive way to be with that means. Furthermore when we reach the actual point of carrying out those desires *for life*, our passions will not work against us, others or life itself. By this completed process we see the evidence of a flow of life, natural and universal as any individual could choose to relate with his or her physical world in this manner.

*THE ELEMENTS OF HEAVEN*

# *In Balance*

Become a means for sharing
Splendid love
Faithfully

Though other truths I include
In happiness complete
I shan't forego the reality
The truth of what you are to me

Remain a means
Never could another
Be my source
Naturally

I would not
In some cerebral ploy
Attempt a transformation
Where you become the personification
Of something I enjoy

Save me not
Yet stay forever
Together for mellifluent life
Nothing can confute this sense
Our ways and means reach congruence

As we have discussed various aspects of ways and means we can now explore certain essential elements of life itself. Preservation of life is a basic principle of existence. Thusly we can follow the formula through making that ideal the "[}**Li**" or "for life" goal. As:

An individual creatively finds a way to incorporate a means for the preservation of his or her life, or an aspect of it. Gaining the means itself would be the *fulfillment* for that particular purpose. The farmer who ingenuously worked with his neighbors, providing for some and hiring others, helped to preserve life by accomplishing a needed goal. Perhaps the idea came to him as he looked out over the fertile expanse of his home. The stark absence of others who could be help for him, might have served as a stimulus for the creative resolution that he employed.

If while in meditation we uncover a missing essential, that which we would need in order to make our lives more complete, we could find or choose a way to include a means for that purpose. Some omitted aspects of life are not that obvious. Like a vitamin deficiency or the lack of one essential part, that which is not there in life is less noticeable than that which is. We can easily see the standing forest but a fallen tree is not as simple to spot. If that which was missing in our lives was affecting us adversely and existed in the physical world, we would need three pieces of knowledge in order to solve the puzzle. The first would be to recognize that there *was* an absence.

*We need to know the Question before we can effectively search for the Answer*

Secondly we would have to be able to identify what the actual absence was. Third we would need to know or find a way to reach and relate to the actual thing, in order to satisfactorily include it into our lives.

With an understanding that wholeness is fulfillment and fulfillment is joy we could look to see how or why we do not feel fulfilled, if this is what we are experiencing. This meditation requires a clear focus because of two relevant issues concerning the location of the "missing piece". It could be either Internal or External. It might be the *way* we are doing or not doing something, making the resolution an internal change. Or it might be that we haven't found the right means, which would place the answer in our exterior environment. A method of meditation that I have used for this regard and metaphorically likening this search to our contemplation of a flower we would know when to:

*Study the flower's roots or openly view the blossom*

Whether we ourselves are the root of the problem, or we need to include another in our *botte de fleurs* making our bouquet of Life more complete. Although we cannot make another our source of happiness, we might be overlooking the Beauty and wonder in the people around us. Therefore Meditation offers itself as a way for the realization of each formula. The blossoms that are waiting to be seen and recognized might hold the very means for the fulfillment we are seeking.

THE ELEMENTS OF HEAVEN

# *The Fullness Thereof*

Luminous, voluptuous
He marvels on feminine beauty
Sinuous, precious
She is pleasure's promise to be
Oh! How he expects ecstasy

Bold, providing
Sinew's strength unfurled
She studies while deciding
If his gifts toward her be hurled

They meet, relate, without confiding
That he does ecstasy await
As she expects the world

Listen brothers
Hearken friends
Beware the gilded light that sends
Your life apace towards ecstatic ends

Milady heed
Illusion's seed
Will not fulfill
Your true dream's need

She is not paradise incarnate
Though we may walk within, with her
He is not the world manifest, yet
Discover Eden follow thither

Know your minds
See your dreams
The gilt road leads not where it seems
Seek first Utopia within meditation
Lest disappointment's rage follows
Ecstasy's vain expectation

\* \* \*

As a Univernatist the method(s) I use (and advocate) for meditation differ mainly from many of the "standard and practiced" disciplines which are taught. Most teachers of meditative techniques encourage and affirm one or more of these three principles:

1) Learning "positions" for meditation such as the *Lotus*...etc. (which can be awkward, uncomfortable and seemingly unnatural disciplines)

2) Clearing the Mind of all thoughts (to serve the meditative process)

3) The constant and continuous repetition of Mantras (esp. those arcane phrases which are indicative of the particular branch of meditation being taught)

What Univernatism promotes, even within formal and forms of meditation, is a type of psychespiritual method which helps and is productive for:

1) Individuals *finding* their important questions (i.e. the issues which are most relevant to them presently)

2) The (balanced) *raising* of the unconscious mind (a vital process for self-discovery and even Enlightenment)

3) Becoming Natural and Universal, individually, hence: the True Self

The way(s) in which these goals are served and met are, I believe, quite natural and scientific:

1) To begin with make yourself *comfortable*, finding the most relaxed position( lying down, sitting with your feet up, reclining on a couch etc…)

I consider that Meditation should *feel* natural; this in of itself helps Natural development and evolution.

2) *Allow yourself to think* (attempting to clear the mind of thoughts can, I believe, be not only unhealthful but actually impossible for many)

3) Without (necessarily) using Mantras let yourself think but learn to: *let go of thoughts*. That is, finding a comfortable position let your consciousness flow, allow thoughts (and feelings) to come to you, as they do: *Think it (or feel it) and Let it go*. I believe that *eventually* you'll come to a thought or point that you *cannot let go of*. That Contemplation, the one that stays with you, the one you are unable to release, is *indicative of a relevant* point, idea, thought and/or situation which you (personally) need to consider and explore.

One can engage in this type of meditation almost anywhere and at anytime he or she is not actively involved in some external situation requiring mental concentration i.e. having a conversation with someone else, or reading etc.

By allowing yourself to think, and *not* purposefully, premeditatedly considering a "subject" your Inner Self will let you know what is really important to you presently. That idea, memory or "inner vision" that you are unable to release is the *Door* to your inward needs that are calling to you.

By following the method(s) of psychespiritual meditation in Univernatism one will gain much insight into his or her inner-self and life itself. Each of our *inner-teachers* (in Eastern thought this is called the "inner-guru") knows us very well, better than we (consciously) know ourselves, therefore by opening the door and developing a clear and insightful relationship with this inner guide, each of us can benefit greatly.

By letting go of the mundane and superfluous thoughts that can occupy our minds and confound our (real) dreams and delving into our important and wise inward searching using the principles described we each will grow towards Selfhood and individual self-realization.

After an important and essential subject or issue is *raised* in Meditation the following outline can be utilized for locating and understanding the crux and true meaning/import of the matter. Being able to discern exactly *Why* this thing is so important to us is key the resolution of it and the furthering of our self-knowledge.

\* \* \*

Justice is another important and often undeniable aspect of life. If we believe that we were treated unjustly, or note various injustices in our lives we will be motivated to address and redress these circumstances. Not receiving our fair share, or truly deserved credit can have an effect on our waking lives.

The anger or resentment we might feel, and think about, could interfere with our everyday demeanor and joy. Obviously we should not physically lash out at those we deem responsible for injustice. Aside from the municipal laws that make physical retribution illegal, most of us have enacted our own laws that keep us from resorting to such base and unnecessary actions. But some things *can* be done. To begin with we should always support ourselves in circumstances such as these; we need to be our own benefactors when others act against our best interests. We should not, especially in situations where injustice is taking place, act against ourselves and compound the problem.

If the persons involved are not open to honestly looking into themselves, or the situation itself, even after we have brought the unjust events to their attention, there are still effective ways in which we could deal with this experience. To begin with, an understanding of the importance and validity of *not making things worse* can be quite useful. Often those who are culpable of these offences are co-workers, acquaintances or people that we see fairly often and have a relationship with. We talk to them and share part of our experiences with them, which may be exactly how the injustice took place. Perhaps they revealed something we shared with them that we had not wished to be repeated. Or they act in a somewhat haughty fashion, disrespectfully "raising themselves up" while we are honestly relating with them. We would be perceived as accepting or endorsing their unwarranted and unjust behavior if we continued to be open and friendly towards them. We need not be overtly rude either, that would be a "taking away" and unnecessary. I have dealt with situations such as these by: *not initiating conversation.* I was neither rude nor disrespectful, I responded politely when greeted, but nothing more. I did not go out of my way to talk with certain individuals or share my experiences with them. I offered perfunctory comments when necessary to get work done, or some need met, calmly, inoffensively but briefly. It does not take that long for this "message" to get received. Once our grievances are brought out into the open using this method or way, a candid and productive conversation usually follows. At this point we can explain fairly but firmly what has been bothering us and save or start an honest relationship. In truth, I have made some lifelong friends by respecting myself in this way.

In another situation we might find ourselves confronting a cacophony of unlike ideas where we find that we cannot relate to many words that are being spoken around us. Perhaps it is at a family gathering where that one in-law is not too subtly expressing opposing or personally offensive views about life. To be rude or insulting towards a relative is never a recommended or acceptable way to comport ourselves. We might not seek to address the conversation directly either, for this would further involve us. A similar situation might unfold at our place of employment or in a friendly social setting. We need not openly confront those who have aggressive or extremely contrary views about life, if we can reasonably foresee that our input will have little or no effect on their opinions. Realizing that by involving ourselves personally in an offensive discussion could only make things worse, we would be wise to remain silent or stay a non-participant. But how could we deal with this event effectively?

If we can understand the *nature* of the problem, the "real question" involved, we will be able to offset the difficulties. Is the whole trouble contained in the fact that some person or persons are aggressively airing viewpoints we find offensive? Or is our *reaction* to this event part of the predicament, even the central part. Not that we would be wrong in reacting with annoyance to a distasteful conversation, but why must we subject ourselves to such? Furthermore, in our understanding of **Sce** ≅ **W+M[}Li** we are Self-creative individuals, in touch also with our first cousin: Love. Then this would be the actual and verifiable crux of the problem: the situation is inadvertently keeping us from our Inner Creativity and Love. The unnecessary cacophony in the world about us, during this event, is posing a problem for our inner goodness, or our philosophies towards Love.

We cannot support a critical judgment of those about us who are ignorant of the realities of Love, for: (negative) *criticism is an act of ignorance*. Thus as we explore even the *crux* of the problem, there exists a central point here to. The actual cause for our reaction of annoyance, which keeps us from being in touch with our inner self, does *not* originate in the external world. Rather it comes from us being annoyed with *ourselves* for allowing such an event to distract us from the Beauty of Love. If we think critically and unfairly judge those around us, we are not being Self-creative and loving. Neither would we be creatively contemplating in a moment such as this. The combination of self-annoyance and loss of creative focus are the real problems in this scenario. Both difficulties can be dealt with and prevented effectively if we were to: *Tune out without turning off.* I have personally found this method of meditation most helpful.

By "tuning out" we mentally and emotionally *disallow* the situation to affect us internally, where our inner creative strength rests. By not "turning off" we remain *with* our inward Love and prevent exterior aggression from making us aggressive. Here then we would be continuing Self-creativity as we connect with a way of preventing a means (in the case the "means" would be an external negative influence) from affecting us adversely.

*Those who you do not respect you need not disrespect*

Before we were able to tune out or even block out physical unpleasantness and negativity, these interlopers could have entered our psyches and lives. We might have been in (close) contact with some people who take away from others and did so to us, when we were unable to prevent this. The act of taking away either from belittling another or projecting unfair criticism upon another can have negative internal effects on the person subjected to these actions. Here an individual's sense of justice is piqued especially when they are older and can defend themselves. At a more capable or authoritative point in their lives they might turn defense into offense and "do that which was done to them". One would need to recognize this type of vicarious revenge and study the root of the problem. Seeking revenge and seeking justice are two very different things.

*Revenge is an act of selfishness,*
*while Justice serves the Self and others as well*

If we understand a basic principle in the creation of *personality* that: *whatever goes in will come out* we could recognize those aspects of us that are not really our true Natures. Some negative traits could be due to external influences that we seek to rid ourselves of. If we were rejected, we might act out and reject others. The criticisms that entered into our psyches because we were unable to mentally stave them off, can turn around within us, and come out towards others. We can and should learn to deal with these artificial aspects of us by: *Working them out, not bringing them out* for the sake of our Natural, real and true selves. In the last chapter we had discussed ways and means for evolving into more loving individuals, now we can explore ideas about our Natural and Genuine individuality. I see "Self with others" as an exemplary way for existence. This paradigm for society or civilization would exclude selfish and destructive personality traits while including those elements of life that are actually our natural inclinations. Thus if we were freed from external negative influences that caused us to be what we are (truly) not, this would be one important step towards naturalness.

With the formula **Sce** $\cong$ **W+M[}Li** Self is understood to be Source, creative. The word source could be seen as synonymous with authority, as an "authority" is a source of knowledge about a certain subject. If we have risen in life to be an authority of some sort, either about a documented subject, or an authority in charge of people or place because of our accrued knowledge and experience, how do we conduct ourselves, personally? If an authority is a source then we should not be dominating or controlling, a source is creative. In these statements we can see an example of the difference between a conditioned or "normal" personality, and a natural one. It can be accepted, as a normal part of the job, for our boss or authority to be dominant, but is this natural? We can evolve past this type of personality and become a natural source, benefiting all those involved, including us. It is neither pleasant nor joyful to dominate another, and it is not necessary either. Self with others describes a creative relationship that is both natural and harmonious, and therefore joy promoting.

Often when a doctor, a lawyer or similar esteemed professional is asked "who they are" they would reply: "I am a physician, a scientist, a psychiatrist, etc." But this is what they *do* not *who* they are. They are, in essence, themselves. What we are could only be accurately answered if we were to explain our Natures, not our professions. A writer is not what I am it is one of the things I enjoy doing. As we explore this common rhetorical response in life, we can actually see some underpinnings of normal and conditioned behavior that is against individual naturalness. For if someone were to truly believe that this is what they really were, we can wonder just how much this is taken literally, and that their lives and personalities could be explained in textbooks. A doctor does and does not do this. A lawyer does and does not do thus, and so on. It could be that the physicians and other respected professionals feel more comfortable when dressed as such, in their respective offices, than when they are standing naked and natural. We need to learn to feel and grow most comfortable with our true natures, for this is what we truly are. Each of us can reach deeper into ourselves, past what our valued and relevant book learning has taught, towards the depth of our Humanity. That is where our own Truths and Joy rest.

Different individuals enjoy different activities; each of us has our own particular pastime and recreation we choose to engage in. As our inner natures tell *what* we are, parts of life that we appreciate are some of the components that can reveal *who* we are. "I am the type of person who enjoys a serious conversation in a quiet surrounding". "I love to be out-of-doors and active, too much thinking and talking bores me". Either of these declarations could have been expressed by someone who did know "who they were", their genuine personalities. "I hate it when someone shows me that I am wrong". "I can't stand people who are freer than me; who do they think they are anyway?" Aggressive comments such as these could be seen as coming out from some inward conflict. When we *do know* who we really are, within, we are less affected by external negative stimulus. With the knowledge and awareness of who we are, as Self, comes an inward strength and power that can fend off unwanted influences while we remain whole and intact. The beauty and potential for creative happiness that exists within our natural personalities makes the difficult task of reaching what and who we truly are worth it. This quest for joy is neither impossible nor impractical, as we all have plenty of time and energy we can devote to ourselves and to our individual lives.

*Liberation is the art of knowing oneself*

Socrates held the belief that a philosopher does not actually teach truth, he saw himself more as the stimulator or catalyst for the truths that rest dormant within each of us. By utilizing the Socratic method, probing the conscious onion of his students, as one layer of questions led to a deeper level, he showed a way for each to explore their own selves. This type of Self with others method that he developed gained for him both praise and punishment, as his students loved what the normal society at that time loathed. He felt that true goodness was natural not theological, that the Virtues of living are learned from within us, not from the lectures or lecterns around us.

With Knowledge as the Liberator, our understanding of those truths that rest beneath the surface layer of life, will afford freedom for us. As we learn to discern just where to step, where not to, and why not to, we are each guided by our inner wisdom. Once we realize that we are not the center of the Universe and that the world does not really revolve around our personal likes and dislikes we might be able to catch a glimpse or two of an actual Intelligent Order. Though not that physically obvious, the sense and systems within the Universe, Nature and Life itself are of a symmetry that we can each tap into and benefit from. By working with and through $Sce \cong W+M[\}Li$ we can reach an ordered freedom which creates balance, not barriers, showing us a course, not chaos. There exists the quality of freedom in Self with others for the relationships therein are formed as purpose, not possession. Beginning from our inner creativity we can reach out our hands and happiness embracing others without keeping them back. We can encourage both friends and lovers to grow with us as we each seek the answers to our questions within, and the solutions to the puzzles that life itself poses for us.

Thus by incorporating the Ideal of Freedom in the [}**Li** outcome we can work to create and maintain our personal liberties, yet remain with others, not isolated. We would not say that a shipwrecked survivor on an unknown atoll was free. Although there would be no others to obey, or appointments to keep, the enisling circumstances of a life apart would in itself be a confinement. Neither is the wanderer lost in the woods actually free. Though his movements would be unrestricted by social regimen there would be no sense of purpose and he would be confined to merely seeking survival. Perhaps ohe day while resting beneath an aged oak, he would hear or see the wisdom of the roots, showing him the way out, and with. Whether we choose to follow our own insights and act upon those ideas that are creative within us is partly a decision of our free will and mostly the determination of our free minds; for indeed the secret of Life is to enjoy It, therefore the meaning of existence is to learn how.

*So this then's the secret of existence*
*Enjoy Life's multiplicity*
*All things have got their point and place*
*For contributing to felicity*

## Queen of Atlantis

The throne was wrought with precious ore
Which was mined in the valleys and hills
Inlaid with gems of flawless crystal
Beveled by artisan's skills
The footstool made of the rarest wood
From the trees of the mythical forest
There one finds midst coniferous pines
Sacred deer at their frolicking best
Showing white coats as soft as the clouds aloft
They made the cushions and headrest

About the palace a garden grew
A velvet lawn meandering
The mirthful trees of revelry
Around the grounds were heard
Their long thin leaves bore oval holes
Through which the breezes passed
Creating the sound of laughing souls
The amusement was unsurpassed

Far above an airjet soared
Which could harness the atoms of light
Built from a mystical science

## THE ELEMENTS OF HEAVEN

It could fly from the Moon at night
If the Luna was new, by the starshine it flew
But then without the same speed
Since levitation was known
To every person full-grown
This made little difference indeed

Atop the Northwing of the castle
Perched a Golden-Throated condor
Causing conversation
This was truly a creature of lore
A bird of particular splendor
Illegal to capture or kill
With multi-colored plumage
And a deep yellow line 'neath its bill
But she remained unimpressed with this
Nothing could rival her beauty
For she was the queen of all Atlantis
She ruled her realm with certainty

From shore to shore her word was law
Guiding the greatest on earth
Atlantis was regality
Her crown was the right of her birth
The ancestry of the royal tree
Dated back nigh the roots of creation

Through all the years Atlantis remained
A strong and unified nation

Full of laughter and enchantment
Were the children Atlantis bred
Learning the ways of wisdom
Through games and legends read
They played in the fields of clover
Which in every color grew
Living myths of history over
Letting the ancient live anew

Their education was invaluable
Thus sundry subjects were given
Students were lettered and laudable
Fine lines of knowledge were woven
Philosophy, science, mathematics
Art and language and speech
Even mystical dynamics
Were the masters told to teach

Astrology was ever important
To determine a child's promise
The position of the planets
Could foretell a scion's genius
"When first we are created

## THE ELEMENTS OF HEAVEN

The universe plants its seeds"
This doctrine was widely stated
As a guide unto children's needs

The builders of Atlantis
Were all masters of a craft
Like their enigmatic children
They created and they laughed
For work was parents' pleasure
Labor was delight
Their days were ruled with measure
Reflection ruled their night

For the smiths of every calling
One principle rang true
Followed without failing
A royal doctrine too
Her Highness had written the statement
To the workers of the realm
"Learn the trade and the enjoyment
Put contentment at your helm"

To the impressionable apprentice
Was this credo ever taught
Into the eager-minded novice
Was labor's wisdom brought

Insightful indeed, and a science
For joyful workers would grow
To reach celerity and excellence
Increasing their output, and so
Atlantis would surely benefit
Its people and markets would thrive
By teaching the ways of this tenet
The quality of life would survive

Like the jewels in the royal tiara
Gleamed the scholars of Atlantis
There were none more enlightened nor rarer
They shed radiance for Her Highness
Venerated, sought for and trusted
Heavenly bodies incarnate
They were the guides and guards for the Kingdom
Their words ever clear, immaculate
The scientist and the magician
The philosopher, magi and each
Esoteric, mysterious illuminate
Ready to tell or teach

Showing the people truthfulness
Lighting the pathway to peace
Exponents of virtue, justness

## THE ELEMENTS OF HEAVEN

Figures for ascent and release
Although they were Atlantis' finest
Shining in all places high
Their limits anon loomed obvious
When faced with an adamant sky

For fate is the final Power
No lesson is greater than She
Soon comes the foreboding hour
Of Atlantis' destiny
With an ephemeris and an astrolabe
The astronomers studied the signs
With the exacting quadrants aid
They followed the orbital lines
The conclusions were unanimous
There was no final escapement
The collective minds of Atlantis
Could not prevent the imminent

The Queen summoned the scientists to Her
To hear of the math in the skies
"It seems that the great planet Titan
Which orbits the Sun after Mars
Is soon to be in conjunction
With Jupiter and because
Of Saturn's particular position

The gravitational sum will cause
Much geophysical division
Those are the natural laws"

"Earth will survive the occurrence
But Titan will not we insist
And Atlantis as we have known her
Will surely cease to exist"

Thus the Queen faced the ultimate challenge
Endure destruction's trumpet
But keep mayhem from the Kingdom
For the sake of historic spirit
She sought for an inspiration
That would move chaos to acceptance
She needed intervention
To keep solace in existence

Atlantis being the pinnacle
The crown of civilization
Must ever preserve her knowledge
For humanities elevation
This was the Queen's final edict:
Protect what is known for Man
By the powers of the mystic
And the Universal plan

## THE ELEMENTS OF HEAVEN

Secure the knowledge in a sphere
Within the ocean's deepness
Write wisdoms secrets in the clouds
Safeguarded for those of goodness
Vouchsafed to keepers of Oneness
Who can see beyond the shrouds

Then the room was filled with smiles
Solemn albeit they were
All praised the Queen of Atlantis
And bowing, acknowledged her

In a sense she had saved the Kingdom
For its learning remains alive
The quintessence alight in wisdom
By its truth it shall survive

Atlantis resides forever
She exists to guide and teach
Forget her lessons never
Her love is yours to reach

www.ingramcontent.com/pod-product-compliance
Lightning Source LLC
Chambersburg PA
CBHW050828160426
43192CB00010B/1937